TEACHER'S HANDBOOK

The SPOKEN WORD Project

TEACHER'S HANDBOOK

Richard Brown

Oliver & Boyd

Oliver & Boyd
Longman House
Burnt Mill
Harlow
Essex CM20 2JE
An Imprint of Longman Group UK Ltd

First published 1989
Third impression 1990
ISBN 0 05 004252 1
Set in Monotype Lasercomp 10/12 Century Schoolbook
Produced by Longman Group (FE) Ltd
Printed in Hong Kong

Contents

Teacher's Notes for Pupils' Book 3: Talk it Through

Developing the spoken word in the primary school

It has long been recognised that children learn through purposeful discussion and in the process develop skills in the use of the spoken word. In 1975 the Bullock Report, *A Language for Life*, touched on the importance of this:

> . . . primary school children spend more time discovering for themselves and talking about their discoveries. The teacher's role in this is vitally important and very demanding; for it is not enough to assume that, given a wide range of activities in a lively primary classroom, the child's language can be left to take care of itself. . . . (10.10)

In the next paragraph it elaborates on the teacher's role in this:

> The teacher's role should be one of planned intervention, and his purposes and the means of fulfilling them must be clear in his mind. Important among these purposes should be the intention to increase the complexity of the child's thinking, so that he does not rest on the mere expression of opinion but uses language in an exploratory way . . . The teacher must devise situations in which the pupils will naturally adopt the kind of behaviour he wants to encourage. In other words, he must structure the learning so that the child becomes positively aware of the need for a complicated utterance, and is impelled to make it. (10.11)

As so much else in the Bullock Report, these points are as relevant now as when they were written. However, their importance was to a great extent overshadowed by comments and recommendations concerning the more established areas of literacy, reading and writing. A great deal of effort went into producing resources for developing reading and writing skills to embody Bullock's ideas; but because so little work had been done in the field of the spoken word, and because there was a strong tradition in many classrooms that pupils should 'stop talking and get on with their work' few resources appeared for this aspect of language development.

Developments did occur, however. Perhaps the most influential was the work carried out by Joan Tough for the Schools Council Communications Project. This examined young children's use of speech and classified it into distinct groups of utterances. It was designed to increase awareness of the range and importance of children's talk; it was not, however, a teaching resource.

Primary language textbooks were slower in reflecting the need for stimulating talk material, and until recently few publishers have given it major attention. It is not surprising, then, that in 1986 the HMI report, *English from 5–16: The Responses to Curriculum Matters 1*, noted that while there was general recognition of the importance of the spoken word by most of those who responded to their original paper, '. . . the responses seldom added suggestions for its development and some noted that it was an area upon which teachers would need assistance.' (31)

This course is an attempt to meet some of the resource needs of teachers in the primary years who want to give more central importance to the development of children's spoken language skills. Its rationale and the way it integrates with the literary curriculum can best be summed up by a paragraph in the HMI document referred to earlier:

> For the classroom teacher, the important points to carry over into daily practice are: that the spoken word should feature as a natural and substantial part of learning; that both talking and listening should usually be integrated; that they should frequently occur in conjunction with other language modes (reading and

writing) and that, wherever possible, they should be employed for 'real or realistic purposes' in the curriculum . . . (32. iii)

Mention has been made of Tough's influential work. Of more recent influence is the pioneering work done by the Government's Assessment of Performance Unit in the early eighties on assessing children's spoken word skills, as reported in *Language Performance in Schools: 1982 Primary Survey Report*. This shows ways of measuring children's oral ability, and the range of speech children use, and indicates the kinds of tasks which demand exploratory and complex utterances and thinking aloud. Schools were issued with a summary document of this work *Speaking and Listening: Assessment at Age 11* which concluded thus:

> It is likely that pupils' performance could be substantially improved if they were given regular opportunities in the classroom to use their speaking and listening skills over a range of purposes, in a relaxed atmosphere. Teachers might consider whether increasing opportunities to take part in talk – in informal and formal contexts, with different types of audience, and for a variety of communicative goals – might increase pupils' awareness of and control over their own speaking and listening practices, and develop their confidence in conveying ideas and points of view in speech. (Page 47)

No published course could or should try to create all the 'opportunities to take part in talk – in informal or formal contexts . . .' and few teachers would expect that; however, one of the main aims of this course is to provide a range of stimulating material to develop a range of discussion skills and to provide models for group discussion which could usefully be applied in other areas of the curriculum.

The APU booklet concludes with an important point about the relationship between talk and learning, which further underpins the importance of developing spoken word skills:

> There is also evidence from research that gains made in mastery of spoken language may have beneficial effects on pupils' learning capabilities. The experience of expressing and shaping ideas through talk as well as writing, and of collaborating to discuss problems or topics, helps to develop a critical and exploratory attitude towards knowledge and concepts. (Page 47)

There is, then, a large measure of agreement about the place of spoken word activities in the primary classroom.

The principles on which this course is based

These are summarised as follows:

1 The development of spoken language cannot be left to itself; planned teacher intervention is necessary.

2 Learning activities devised by the teacher should in the main lead to spoken language which is exploratory and relatively complex.

3 There should be a sufficient variety of activities to develop a range of types of spoken language; these should be interesting, relevant and purposeful, not devised merely for testing and assessment.

4 Learning through the spoken word should have parity with the development of reading and writing.

5 Spoken word activities should be a regular part of classroom learning.

6 Talking and listening are seen as integral skills.

7 Talk between peers is likely to improve pupils' awareness of and control over their own speaking and listening practices.

8 Talk is likely to give pupils greater confidence and skill in conveying their own ideas, opinions and feelings.

9 The gains made in mastery of spoken language may have beneficial effects on pupils' learning capabilities.

10 Paired and small group work – which this course favours – will increase the pupils' ability to work collaboratively and cooperatively and develop respect for other points of view.

11 Spoken word activities do not always have to serve the needs of other learning activities but can in themselves be valuable starting points for learning from which other activities may develop.

12 The teacher's role is as a manager and coordinator of the activities; his/her views are not dominant; he/she sets the scene, facilitates the group discussion, draws the various threads together and clarifies any outstanding points.

13 Discussion among peer groups is the favoured form of learning in this course. The teacher is not expected to lead the discussion. Studies have shown that where the teacher is dominant in discussion, pupils' utterances are often restricted, infrequent and not exploratory. For some teachers this will be a departure from normal practice and may be difficult to effect at first. That is why detailed notes on how to organise and carry out the activities are provided in this guide.

14 This course is not designed to develop formal performance skills – such as giving speeches and recitations – although some activities might include elements of these.

15 The work done by the APU in assessing children's oral ability is fascinating, but it is, as I write, still in the early stages of development. Paradoxically, it has convinced me that it is unrealistic to expect the ordinary, busy primary teacher to attempt assessment of individual pupil's spoken word skills in anything but the most simple, empiric way. The APU assessments of individual pupil's performance were made by trained assessors who used a combination of analytic and impressionistic marking systems, recorded tapes, case conferences, etc. – a time-consuming and complicated business almost impossible for the class teacher to replicate. Therefore, in the absence of a well-tried practical system of assessment easy to operate, this course does not expect teachers to make detailed assessments of individual pupil's spoken word skills. A number of measurable things could, however, be noted. For example:

(a) Does the pupil willingly join in the group discussion?

(b) Does the pupil take in other points of view?

(c) Can the pupil change his/her initial view after discussion, if this seems appropriate?

(d) Is the pupil a good listener?

(e) Is the pupil able and willing to report to you and/or the rest of the class on what has been said in the group?

(f) Does the pupil's behaviour in any way inhibit or disrupt the group's discussion? If so, what can be done about it?

(g) Does the pupil show any weakness in using a particular type of spoken language, e.g. narrative?

(h) What is the pupil's general attitude to group discussion: enthusiastic/interested/indifferent/antipathetic?

A record sheet of the activities used with the pupils can, however, be useful, and a specimen one is supplied at the end of this introduction. It may be photocopied for classroom use. It is intended that in the small boxes containing diagonal lines the teacher will enter the date and the activity number used in the appropriate column. Like this:

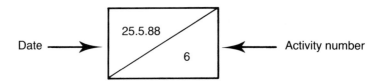

This will show what activities in this course the pupil has had experience of, show other staff and parents and facilitate continuity of work when the pupil's next teacher takes over.

16 Finally, teachers should recognise that the social context in which the child is discussing will have an effect on his performance. As the APU booklet *Speaking and Listening* referred to earlier, notes:

Speakers are always influenced by contextual factors such as:

* who they are talking to
* where the interaction takes place
* how they interpret the nature of the task
* how they interpret the motivations and intentions of their conversational partners or their audience, and therefore
* the nature of the feedback they get. (Page 3)

The teacher will need to recognise these contextual influences when using the material and assessing the performance of the pupil.

Using the pupils' course book material

The material is a collection of ideas organised into three levels to take into account the differing needs of lower, middle and upper juniors. It is not organised in a linear or progressive structure, and therefore this allows the teacher to pick and choose any of the activities which he/she thinks is the most likely to appeal to his/her pupils. However, the teacher's notes do make an attempt to note the kind of talk the activity is expected to develop and this may be a factor in the choice. For example, the teacher may wish to concentrate on persuasive talk; if so, he/she can pick out those activities which develop this by referring to the index at the end of the pupils' course books and use them in succession. The activities often have subsidiary aims and these are spelt out in the *objectives* section of the notes; these, too, might help in the choice of the activities to use. If the teacher is currently running a project which is the subject of one or more of the activities, then it would make sense to link the two.

Every activity in the pupils' books is accompanied by detailed teacher's notes in this guide. Experienced and/or imaginative teachers may find these notes too prescriptive; they can, of course, ignore or modify them as seems appropriate.
It is hoped, however, that such detail will be of more assistance to those for whom group discussion work of this nature is unfamiliar.

   Most of the notes follow a set pattern:
(a) Talk expected
(b) Objectives
(c) Preparation
(d) Organisation
(e) Extension

These are discussed below.

(a) Talk expected

Different researchers come up with different labels for types of talk; there is no standard taxonomy of speech utterances. I have tried to use terms which are part of everyday speech, but they will of course need defining:

PERSUASIVE: Putting forward and developing a point of view with the aim of persuading the listener to adopt or at least concede that point of view. Subsumed within this category is ARGUMENTATIVE, which is a little different in that it implies *defending* a point of view rather than extending it to others.

PREDICTIVE: making predictions about future events, and anticipating likely developments.

COMPARATIVE: comparing different ideas or positions in order to reveal their merits and meanings.

IMAGINATIVE: projecting into other realities, creating mental images and conveying this to others.

DESCRIPTIVE: saying what something looks, feels, tastes, sounds and/or smells like.

NARRATIVE: constructing or retelling a story.

INTERPRETATIVE: speculating about and assigning meanings to words and actions whose meaning is ambiguous or not known.

PERSONAL: talking about personal concerns, the inner realities of feelings, aspirations, dreams, fears, beliefs, etc.

INSTRUCTIVE: giving instructions and directions for a listener to act upon.

EXPLANATORY: making something known in detail and saying what is meant.

QUESTIONING: asking questions to elicit information.

REPORTING: saying what has happened.

These are not scientifically precise definitions but it is hoped they will be readily understood and of use in planning what activities to use with the pupils. They all appear on the suggested record sheet which appears at the end of this introduction. Also on the record sheet are the terms DIALECT and PERFORMANCE SKILLS. The latter term refers to skills involved in reading aloud, playing a part, giving a prepared speech, etc.

   At the back of the pupils' course books there is an index of spoken word types. Some types are represented more than others, and this needs to be taken into account when seeking to create a balance of different activities, e.g. Book 1 has few of the EXPLANATORY type, and Book 2 has few PERSONAL or INSTRUCTIVE; these gaps will need filling elsewhere.

(b) Objectives

Teachers need to have good, rational, educational reasons for the learning situations they set up, and so an attempt has been made to define the objectives of each of the pupils' activities. Again, these by their nature cannot be scientifically precise but should be of use in helping to understand the point of the activities.

(c) Preparation

This has a two-fold function. There is the functional one which indicates the materials and equipment needed to carry out the activity; and there is the contextual one which has suggestions for introducing the activity and creating a context for it.

(d) Organisation

This is a point by point suggestion of how you might carry out the lesson. As mentioned earlier, experienced and imaginative teachers may well wish to ignore or depart from the suggested approach to suit their own ideas and situation; others may wish to follow it more closely and make modifications in the light of experience. Such detailed lesson notes may not be usual in textbook courses of this kind, but were felt to be necessary for those teachers for whom discussion activities of this type are unfamiliar.

(e) Extension

This section suggests logical developments of the discussion activity and links the work to other areas of the curriculum. It helps to ensure that the course, though a separate thread within the curriculum, is also an integral part of its pattern.

References

APU *Language Performance in Schools: Primary Survey Report 1982*, DES, 1984.
Bullock, A. *A Language for Life*, HMI, 1975.
MacLure, M. and Hargreaves, M. *Speaking and Listening: Assessment at Age 11*, APU/DES, 1986.
HMI *English from 5–16: The Responses to Curriculum Matters I*, DES, 1986.
Tough, J. *Listening to Children Talking*, (1976), *Talking and Learning*, (1977), *Talk for Teaching and Learning*, (1979), Ward Lock Educational.

Other useful references

Brittin, A. *The Spoken Word in the Primary School*, Jordanhill College of Education, 1984.
Sutton, C. *Communicating in the Classroom*, Hodder & Stoughton, 1981.
Wade, B. *Talking to Some Purpose*, University of Birmingham, Educational Review Publication No. 12, 1985.

RECORD SHEET

Pupil's name _____ **Class** _____

Teacher's name _____ **Year** _____

Type of talk expected	Activity number and date							
Persuasive								
Predictive								
Comparative								
Imaginative								
Descriptive								
Narrative								
Interpretative								
Personal								
Instructive								
Explanatory								
Questioning								
Reporting								
Dialect								
Performance skills								

(photocopiable for classroom use only)

Teacher's Notes for

The SPOKEN WORD Project

Book 1:
Talk it Out

(For Lower Junior pupils)

1 Golden Rules for talking in groups

Talk expected: persuasive.

Objectives: to consider with the pupils the best ways of behaving in discussion groups.

Each book in the course begins with this material.

Preparation: You will need a board with chalk or marker to list the best Golden Rules put forward by the pupils. The pupils will need pencil and paper.

Organisation: In pairs, threes or fours pupils discuss and draw up a list of their Golden Rules. They report back and the best are listed on the board.

Extension:
(a) Two groups could act out the differences between a well-behaved discussion group and a poorly-behaved one. The latter would need a little rehearsal time. The rest of the class watching the sketch could note examples of good and bad behaviour and report back on them. Of course, if poor behaviour in discussion groups is not a problem this activity will be unnecessary.
(b) Make a chart of the best Golden Rules for display, as an *aide mémoire*, and to refer to in the future should the pupils need a reminder.

2 To talk about before you start

Talk expected: persuasive; predictive; comparative.

Objectives:
(a) to establish in the pupils' minds the overriding importance of talk as the main form of communication in their lives
(b) to give opportunities for persuasive talk
(c) to consider several points of view.

Preparation: a board with a chalk or a marker will be needed on which to write the groups' results.

Organisation:
(a) Talk a little about ways of communicating with words.
(b) Ask the pupils who taught them to talk, to read and to write. Families will figure large in their responses, particularly with regard to talk.
(c) Emphasise that much time is spent at school developing reading and writing, but less so on developing talking and listening. This book will help them to improve their skills as talkers and listeners.
(d) Put the names of John, Grace and Mui on the board underneath each other.
(e) Read out the opinions on the page. Write TALKING and LISTENING beside John's name, READING beside Grace's name and WRITING beside Mui's.
(f) Ask the pupils to discuss in pairs or threes what they think they will *need most* in their lives: talking, listening, reading, or writing.

(g) Ask each group to report back. Keep a tally on the board of each pupil's view. Views may differ in a group. Question some of the responses to open out the discussion. Talk generally comes out as the favourite.

Extension:
(a) Ask the pupils to talk in their pairs or threes: 'What if you lost your voice for a week? What problems would arise? How would you cope?'
(b) A small group could conduct a survey of their class's own appraisal of their performance in talk. The group could ask each pupil:
Do you think you are
(1) a good confident talker wherever you are?
(2) quite a good talker for most of the time?
(3) a good talker in situations you know and with people you know, otherwise you are shy?
(4) quiet and shy with most people?
The survey could, of course, be done anonymously by passing the questionnaire around the class on a clipboard. The results might give you food for thought.

3 Can you solve this problem?

Talk expected: imaginative; explanatory.

Objectives:
(a) to give an opportunity to solve a problem through discussion
(b) to develop listening by providing picture cues to a text being read aloud
(c) to consider alternative solutions to a problem.

Preparation: Have a board with chalk or marker ready to record the pupils' solutions to the problem.

Organisation:
(a) Split the class into pairs or threes. Make sure each group has a book to follow.
(b) Read aloud the first part of the story.
(c) Without giving any of your own ideas, ask the pupils how they would solve Michael's problem.
(d) Ask each group to report back. Several solutions will probably be forthcoming. List them and then discuss their individual merits.
(e) Read the second part of the story. Ask the pupils' opinion of it. Was it better than any of the solutions already discussed?

The Hollow Post – *Part One*

On a piece of waste land there stood a tall, hollow post. No one quite knew why it was there. The three boys who used the ground for football found the post useful as a goalpost.

Michael was the youngest of the three friends. He could be very quick on the football pitch, even though his kicks were seldom accurate.

Today they were playing football as usual. Michael wove around his opponent and headed towards the goal. He swung his foot. The ball sailed into the air – but far too high! It made a graceful curve and then, amazingly, it fell straight down inside the hollow post.

The boys stood around the post in dismay. Then the eldest said, 'What a duff shot. Why did you kick it so high?'

'Showing off,' the other said.

Michael climbed onto one of his friend's shoulders and peered into the hollow. The ball was so far down in the dark it could only just be seen.

'Can it be fished out with my fishing net?' one of them called.

'No,' Michael shouted back. 'You'd never get it round the ball.'

Michael climbed down. The other two stood in front of him, hands on hips. Although they were his friends, at this moment he felt a little afraid of them.

'You'll have to get another ball. That one belonged to us all, and it's gone for good.'

Michael protested, 'But I haven't got another ball.'

'Then buy one. Use your pocket money.' With that his friends ran off, leaving Michael to count the cost of his wild kick.

Part Two

In a flash an idea came to him.

Near the waste land was a ditch. It had been full of water that morning from the night's heavy rain, and Michael had noticed a bucket sticking out of it. He ran to where the bucket was, leaned over and pulled it out. It was very rusty and it leaked a bit – but it would be good enough for his purpose.

He carried the bucket full of muddy water back to the post. Stacking a few old boxes from the waste ground against the post, he was able to lift the bucket to the lip of the hollow and pour the water in. Back and forth he went to the ditch, carrying pail after pail of water to pour into the post. The ball, floating on the water, rose higher and higher.

By the time he could reach the ball his arms ached and he felt sticky, but that did not spoil his sense of triumph. He eased the wet ball out of the post and with a shout he threw it in the air.

He ran home and then went to find his friends. When he told them how he had done it they whistled in astonishment and called him a genius.

4 Can you share a story book?

Talk expected: descriptive; persuasive.

Objectives:
(a) to give the group a chance to voice their opinions and preferences with regard to sharing books
(b) to encourage them to see reading as a shared activity as well as a solitary one
(c) to encourage them to talk about their books with each other.

Preparation: talk to the class about different reading habits – including your own.

Organisation:
(a) Split the class into pairs or threes.
(b) Read aloud the four views of reading presented.

(c) Ask the pupils: (1) which do they agree with? (2) which best describes their own favoured practice?

(d) Write the names PRITTI, BEN, MARION and ANDREW on the board. Give a point to each for each supporting response from the groups. This will show how the class view this aspect of reading.

(e) Sum up the discussion by drawing up a number of statements about reading, each beginning with 'We like to . . .'.

Extension: You could explore the pupils' reading preferences here. Ask each group to list in order of preference the following kinds of books: pop-up books, picture books, poetry books, story books, factual books, annuals and joke books. A score is assigned to each, ranging from 7 for the first choice to 1 for the last. Tot up the class scores on the board to show the class's preferences.

5 What if . . ?

Talk expected: imaginative; narrative.

Objectives:
(a) to encourage pupils to imagine unusual situations
(b) to provide a stimulus for spontaneous narration.

Preparation: The 'What if . . ?' principle is often used as an imaginative exercise. Some writers – Helen Cresswell, for example – are on record as saying that this is often the way they begin a story. They might ask, 'What if a strange new plant just grew and grew at a fantastic rate?' (In Helen Cresswell's case the answer was a full length novel, *The Bongleweed*.) Talk to pupils about this device which opens up endless imaginative possibilities.

Organisation:
(a) If the whole class is to be involved, split them into pairs and threes and select one of the 'What if . . ?' ideas for discussion.
(b) Generate a discussion with the whole class to give an example of the kind of talk you hope the pupils will engage in in their own groups.
(c) Ask the pupils to choose one of the other ideas for discussion.

Extension:
(a) Some groups might like to record their 'What if . . ?' stories. This could be done in writing, or on tape, or in a sequence of pictures.
(b) Pupils could be encouraged to invent their own 'What ifs . . ?' for discussion. These could be written on cards and gathered together for future work of this kind.
(c) Some of these ideas could form the basis of stories and pictures and improvised drama.

6 Can you make a picture story?

Talk expected: narrative.

Objectives:
(a) to develop spontaneous storytelling
(b) to give pupils the opportunity to make conceptual and imaginative links between unrelated images
(c) to demonstrate that pictures in various combinations can be an effective stimulus for storytelling.

Organisation:
(a) Talk with the pupils about each of the pictures. Suggest potentials of each. For example, the cat could be a favourite pet, or a stray, or a wizard's familiar, or a human in disguise, or magic. . . . Pupils are not likely to think along these lines unless you point out the imaginative possibilities of each picture. However, avoid the temptation to construct a story from them yourself – at least in the pupils' hearing!
(b) Divide the class or group into pairs or threes, each with a book. Let each one in the group work out at least one story.
(c) Ask for volunteers to retell their story to the rest of the class. Encourage the rest of the class to ask the teller questions about the story to make it more explicit.
(d) Suggest that some children make their own sets of picture cards by drawing them or using pictures from magazines, cards, etc.
(e) Encourage pupils to return to this page to make up new stories with a different combination of pictures.

Extension:
(a) Use the same idea in drama, except that pupils act the story.
(b) Use the same idea for story writing. An obvious outcome would be picture books written and drawn by the pupils.

7 What should Sarah do?

Talk expected: imaginative; persuasive.

Objectives
(a) to provide an opportunity for imaginative identification with a character
(b) to provide an open-ended problem for discussion
(c) to give an opportunity for testing and sharing differing viewpoints.

Preparation: Ask the pupils if (a) their mother has been in hospital; how did they feel? and (b) if they have ever been in the situation of desperately wanting to buy their mother a present yet having no money to do so. Whether or not you get any response to these questions, this will lead into the situation portrayed in this 'dilemma tale'.

Organisation:
(a) If individual pairs or threes are going to use this story, ask them to read it for

themselves and report back to you with their views after a thorough discussion. Ask them to consider an alternative solution.
(b) If a larger group or the whole class is to do it at the same time, read them the story and then split them into pairs or threes for discussion.
(c) Make a note on the board of the various solutions.
(d) Be prepared to add any solutions you have thought of which have not been raised.
(e) Finally, ask the groups to reconsider their solution in the light of the others on the board. Take a vote.

Extension: Can any of the pupils make up their own dilemma tale to put to the rest of the class for discussion? Ask them to write it down and give it to you for possible future use.

8 What a riddle!

Talk expected: interpretative.

Objectives:
(a) to provide a stimulus for interpretative discussion
(b) to help pupils reason by referring to supporting details
(c) to stimulate an interest in the riddle form.

Preparation: Explain the nature of riddles.

Organisation:
(a) The first two riddles are easier than the other four so that most pupils beginning this page will meet with quick success and will be introduced to the way riddles work. These two riddles can be done with yourself leading the discussion. Stress that *every* clue must fit the solution offered in order for it to be valid.
(b) Split the class or group into pairs and ask them to solve the remaining four riddles.
(c) When they report back, make sure they can give detailed supporting reasons for their answers. Accept more than one solution for the same riddle if it can be justified. The answers the author has in mind are: (1) a bird, (2) a ball, (3) a sock or boot, (4) a pair of trousers, (5) grass, (6) an elephant.

Extension: Encourage children to write riddles themselves for others to solve.

9 Can you tell a tall story?

Talk expected: narrative.

Objectives: to stimulate storytelling in small groups.

Preparation: Talk about the nature of tall stories: that they are meant to be funny, are full of impossible events and are not to be taken seriously. Some nonsense tales in verse form by Spike Milligan could be used to get the pupils in the mood.

Organisation:
(a) Talk with the class or group about the pictures of Molly and Timothy. Explain that each of Molly's injuries had a separate cause and happened on a different day of the week. Two of the explanations for these injuries are given as models of the kind of tall story you hope the pupils will invent for the rest of the week days.
(b) Read the first two stories aloud. Have a pupil in the class/group read Timothy's part.
(c) Split the class or group into groups of four. Each has to invent an explanation for the other week days. Encourage the pupils to make their stories at least as long as and as detailed and inventive as those already told by Molly.
(d) Invite some pupils to report back on what happened on Tuesday to Friday. Several versions of each day can be given.
(e) Give each group more time to rehearse their Saturday stories. Help those who are struggling. Then invite each group to choose one member to retell their Saturday story – or they can all do it together.
(f) Alternatively, if you find that reporting back to the class is too difficult for some pupils, arrange for them to record their story on tape.

Extension:
(a) Each member of the group could write or make a picture of what happened to Molly. These, together with the accounts already given for Monday and Tuesday could be made into picture books for use with younger children.
(b) If this tall story idea proves popular, invite pupils to repeat it another time with different characters.
(c) Ask pupils to write their own tall stories.
(d) A similar approach to this idea is taken elsewhere in this book: Can you continue the story? (p. 31). You may wish to continue in your next session with that.

10 What do you think of grannies?

Talk expected: personal; comparative; descriptive.

Objectives:
(a) to encourage pupils to talk in a personal and anecdotal way
(b) to give them an opportunity to make comparisons
(c) to stimulate descriptive language.

Preparation: Introduce the theme of this page by asking some pupils to talk about their grandmothers.

Organisation:
(a) Split the class or group into pairs.
(b) Read aloud the two accounts of grandmothers given on this page.
(c) Write on the board as a guide for discussion:
    (1) In what way are these grannies different?
    (2) Describe your grandmother in detail to your partner.
    (3) Make a list of the things you think an ideal granny should be.

(d) Ask some groups to report back on questions (1) and (3). For (3) compile on the board a list of their best suggestions.

Extension:
(a) Ask groups to describe their grandfathers. These discussions could be summarised in drawing and writing.
(b) One group could make a large painting or collage of An Ideal Granny which could be displayed alongside the list of the pupils' suggestions about this compiled earlier.

11 Can you describe something?

Talk expected: descriptive.

Objectives:
(a) to encourage pupils to use descriptive language in which accurate detail is important
(b) to develop visual perception.

Preparation: It may well be better for you to have a bank of pictures ready for this game, especially if a large number of children are going to play it simultaneously. Otherwise, make sure you have plenty of sources of pictures, such as magazines, ready for pupils to begin their own picture search. Also have ready card, spray-glue and scissors.

Organisation:
(a) Divide the class or group into pairs.
(b) Make sure each pair have at least twenty pictures between them.
(c) Explain the intentions behind the game they are going to play, emphasising the importance of accurate descriptive language in daily life.
(d) Explain the rules of the game. Hold up a large picture and demonstrate how clues about it should be given.
(e) Let each pair have a trial run using one picture each.
(f) Ask if any pair has encountered problems. Check that all are quite sure how to play the game.
(g) Begin the game. Circulate to check that it is being played correctly.

Extension:
(a) Ask the pupils to think of as many situations as they can where accurate description might be important.
(b) By using different combinations of pictures, the class or group could play this game several times if it proves popular and successful.

12 What is a proverb?

Talk expected: interpretative; imaginative.

Objectives:
(a) to explore the meanings of some well-known proverbs

(b) to consider several possible alternative meanings for each proverb

(c) to create imaginative situations that illustrate the proverbs' meanings.

Preparation: Talk about the prevalence of proverbs in everyday speech. Give some examples not included on the page. Explain that they are old sayings and are rather like riddles, which are baffling unless you know their meaning. Read out the proverbs given on the pupil's page and ask if any of them are unfamiliar to the children.

Organisation:
(a) Divide the class or group into pairs.
(b) Ask the pairs to consider the meaning of each proverb. Point out the help that the clues can give. The pupils might wish to make notes as a reminder when reporting back.
(c) Ask pairs to report back on at least one of the proverbs. They should give an example of a situation in which the proverb's meaning is illustrated.

Extension:
(a) Each proverb could stimulate a written fable or short story.
(b) Similarly, each proverb could be the literal subject of a picture.
(c) Some pupils might want to collect lists of proverbs from family and friends.

13 The Shrinking of Kate

Talk expected: predictive; interpretative; imaginative.

Objectives:
(a) to stimulate pupils to reflect in a variety of ways on what is happening to characters in a story
(b) to develop listening skills.

Preparation:
(a) Read the story at the end of these particular notes to yourself.
(b) Find a copy of *The Shrinking of Treehorn* by Florence Parry Heide (Puffin) and read it if you have not already done so. Decide whether you want to read the book to the class a few days before or just prior to using this page – it would help the pupils to know what was going through Kate's mind at the beginning of the story. If there is not time to read the book to the pupils, give them a synopsis of it at the beginning of the lesson.

Organisation:
(a) Divide the class into pairs or threes. Make sure each of them can follow the pictures on the page as you read the first part of the story.
(b) Explain that the story is divided into four parts and at the end of each of the first three parts there will be questions for the group to discuss.
(c) Read the first part of the story.
(d) Ask pupils to discuss the questions at the bottom of their page.
(e) Invite some of the groups to report back.
(f) Read the next part of the story. Write the questions for discussion on the board. Continue in this way until you reach the end of the story.

Extension:
(a) Encourage the pupils to talk about Kate's next adventure/problem when she finds herself growing taller and taller. This could lead into written or picture-sequence stories.
(b) Read aloud the parts in *Alice's Adventures in Wonderland* in which Alice shrinks and grows taller alternately.

The Shrinking of Kate – *Part One*

One of Kate's favourite books was called *The Shrinking of Treehorn*. It was about a boy who found that he was getting smaller and smaller. But his parents did not seem to notice!

Kate read this book many times. Then one day she said to herself, 'I wish I could shrink like Treehorn.' Nothing happened – nor did she expect anything to happen – but she repeated her wish six more times that day.

Next morning, when she woke up, everything looked twice as big.

What has happened to Kate?

How did it happen?

What will her mum and dad and little brother Robert say?

What do you think will happen to Kate during the day?

Part Two

You were right, she found she was only half her normal size. She stared at herself in the mirror and was a little afraid. But when she put on her dress she laughed aloud – it was much too big. All her clothes were too big.

She crept into Robert's room. Robert sat up in amazement. 'Sh!' said Kate. 'Can I borrow some of your clothes? Mine no longer fit me.'

Once she was dressed, she felt better.

Now it was time to see what her parents would say. Treehorn's parents hadn't noticed their son's shrinking. Perhaps her parents wouldn't notice hers either.

She pushed open their bedroom door. Mum was reading the paper. Dad was drinking tea.

'Hello,' Kate said uncertainly.

Mum shrieked. Dad spilt his tea all over the bedclothes. They were horrified. Kate was pleased she was getting so much attention, although she was a little sorry that her parents were so upset.

'What shall we do?' her parents wailed to each other.

If you were Kate's parents, what would you do?

What do you think Robert is thinking and feeling while this is going on?

Part Three

Kate's parents rushed her to the doctor. The doctor, however, was a new one; he had never seen Kate before. So he just smiled at her and said, 'She looks perfectly healthy to me.'

'But she's nine years old,' Kate's mum protested.

'Nonsense,' said the doctor. 'I should say she's not more than four and a half. Now I think you are beginning to waste my time . . .'

After that they rushed her down to the hospital – and got the same response.

'Don't make such a fuss,' Kate said when they got home. 'Treehorn got back to his real size.' But they hardly listened to her, they were too perplexed.

The next morning Kate was even smaller. She was now shorter than Robert who was only three years and a bit. Her mum nearly fainted; her dad said he was going to have a heart-attack.

They hid their daughter in her bedroom – what would the neighbours say? Kate got very bored. What could she do? Who could help her get back to her normal size?

One thing was sure – she hated being tiny. Everything had changed in her life.

What has changed in Kate's life? What will she find difficult to do?

How will the story end? If you can, think of a happy ending and then an unhappy ending. Which do you like best?

Part Four

Kate had a great-aunt who lived near by and who thought the world of her. This great-aunt was very clever. She lived on her own in a house full of books.

When night fell, Kate dressed herself in some of her doll's clothes and then jumped downstairs. She had no difficulty in getting outside – she simply climbed through the cat-door. Then she set off for her great-aunt's.

It was so late when she reached the house that her great-aunt was in her dressing gown, ready for bed. When she opened the front door and saw little Kate panting on the doorstep she thought she must be having a nightmare.

Sitting in front of the embers of the living-room fire, Kate's great-aunt thought hard about the problem. She looked in some old books; she shook her head; she frowned and sighed.

Kate fell asleep

When dawn came, even the doll's clothes were too large for Kate. Great-aunt stared at her, tears in her eyes.

Then the telephone rang. It was Robert – the first time he had ever used the telephone on his own. 'Is Kate there?' he asked. Great-aunt said she was. 'She must come back, back, back,' he shouted, and hung up.

The word 'back' echoed in Great-aunt's mind. 'Back' – that was it! Kate must say whatever spell she used backwards – then the spell would work the other way.

She woke Kate and told her what to do. 'Treehorn like shrink could I wish I,' said Kate. She said it seven times. Then she began to grow. In no time at all she grew to her normal size.

As she was walking home, she couldn't resist saying the spell backwards just once more. Immediately she shot up a head taller than she should have been. 'Oh dear,' she said, and giggled.

14 Can you teach something?

Talk expected: instructive; explanatory.

Objectives:
(a) to give pupils the opportunity to use instructive and explanatory language for a real purpose
(b) to develop listening skills
(c) to pass on skills and enthusiasms from child to child.

Preparation: It is unlikely that the whole or a large part of the class will be doing this page simultaneously, so decide which pairs you want to work on it.

Organisation:
(a) Talk about the intentions and expectations of the page. Make sure that one pupil in each pair has a skill to pass on and has the necessary materials to do it.
(b) Emphasise that the pupil *being taught* the new skill will eventually have to show you or another pupil what has been learned.
(c) From time to time check to see that the pairs are working successfully.
(d) When the pair has finished, ask the pupil who is teaching the skill to tell you in the right order what instructions were given.
(e) Encourage the pupil just taught to talk to you about what happened and then to find another partner to pass on the newly learned skill.

Extension: If a number of artefacts result from this activity, display them alongside a list of written instructions drawn up by the pupils.

15 What's the difference?

Talk expected: descriptive; comparative.

Objective: to give the pupils an opportunity to use descriptive and comparative language in a detailed and accurate way.

Preparation: Make sure you have enough dice for each pair to play this game. Decide how many pairs are to play it at the same time. If you have enough dice there is no reason why the whole class could not play it simultaneously.

Organisation:
(a) Read aloud to the class or group the dialogue between Rakesh and Rukshana.
(b) To demonstrate the rules, play the game with a pupil, you throwing the dice and answering the questions.
(c) Let pairs have a trial run. Then stop them to ask if there are any problems.
(d) Later, emphasise the last point made on the pupil's page, about how to make the game more difficult.

Extension: You may wish to progress to the next page – which features the same two characters – at your next session.

16 What am I thinking of?

Talk expected: questioning; descriptive.

Objectives:
(a) to give pupils practice in asking relevant questions and making deductions from the answers given
(b) to give pupils practice in classifying objects
(c) to develop listening and memory.

Preparation: The best way to teach this game is to play it with the whole class first. You think of an object in view, they question you about it. Emphasise the good questions (such as those given on the pupil's page) and those questions that will elicit only very little, specific rather than general, information. For example, a question such as 'Is it bigger than my hand?' if answered 'No', will eliminate a great many possible questions and narrow the range of questions significantly.

Organisation:
(a) Let the pupils have a trial run. Stress the need to keep accurate scores. If it becomes apparent that twelve questions are not enough at the beginning, be flexible about this. Ask if any pair has encountered problems.
(b) Circulate as the pairs play. Listen to the kind of questions being asked. Are they more general than specific?
(c) If the game proves successful it can be made more difficult by asking for objects which are not in view, or even things, such as air, which cannot be seen.

17 Who am I thinking of?

Talk expected: descriptive.

Objectives:
(a) to develop the use of descriptive language
(b) to develop listening
(c) to develop perception and interpretation of visual material.

Preparation: Have some pictures of people in groups ready for a possible follow-up.

Organisation:
(a) Divide the class or group into pairs.
(b) Explain the rules of the game. Give one demonstration. Explain what is meant by 'expressions', 'body positions' and 'personalities' in relation to the picture.
(c) If some groups finish early and wish to continue with this idea, give them another picture of people in a group.

Extension: This game could be played using the pupils in the class as subjects, rather than a picture.

18 Can you continue the story?

Talk expected: descriptive; narrative; predictive.

Objectives: to develop storytelling.

Preparation: Explain that this is a story with vital parts missing which the pupils are challenged to fill in. Have a tape-recorder ready if you want a group to record their work.

Organisation:
(a) Split the class or group into threes or fours.
(b) Read the first part of the story to the pupils while they follow it in their books.
(c) Demonstrate what is required for the first task. For example, to defeat the dragon Nargis could have changed into a marsh into which the dragon sank without trace; to defeat the spider she could have turned into a boulder which rolled down a hill and crushed it.
(d) Circulate and help those pupils who are finding it difficult. *If turn-taking in groups inhibits rather than encourages talk, abandon it in the affected groups and substitute a collective approach.*
(e) When most of the groups have finished, encourage them to repeat their list of events to aid memory.
(f) Ask for some groups to report back on how each danger was overcome.
(g) The next part of the story is as open-ended as it can be and you must judge how much help particular groups will need. Whatever happens in the glass palace will be a self-contained episode in the story, so anything, including new characters, can be invented for it.
(h) The third part of the story uses the idea of a Magic Stone. This differs from the Changing Seed in that the stone itself changes rather than Nargis – so make sure the pupils are aware of this. Repeat points (d)–(f).
(i) The final part is again very open-ended. Ask groups to report back and compare the quality of the endings offered.

Extension:
(a) This idea could well be explored further in drama after the pupils have gone through the exercises above.
(b) It could be a rich source of art work. Large concertina books could be made, with different groups in the class concentrating on one of the four parts of the story. Then each group could use these as visual aids while retelling their part of the story to a new audience in the school.

19 What's the best way?

Talk expected: persuasive; personal; comparative.

Objectives:
(a) to stimulate pupils to consider a number of possible courses of action and to use persuasive language in saying which ones they prefer
(b) to compare the merits of several viewpoints
(c) to encourage pupils to contribute personal anecdotes where these are appropriate.

Preparation: Talk to the pupils about the problem of losing a ball in a neighbour's garden. Several children will, almost certainly, be able to contribute their experience of this.

Organisation:
(a) Read the story to the pupils while they follow it.
(b) Explain that they (in pairs) have to consider *each* of the alternatives given and pick out the ones they prefer.
(c) When the pupils report back, gather several views about each point. You could if you wish ask the whole class to vote on each item to indicate whether they think it would be an effective course of action, recording the results on the board.

Extension:
(a) Write some more dilemma tales yourself, with or without a list of alternatives.
(b) If you have some inventive writers in the class, ask them if they can write a dilemma tale, perhaps based upon a real event.
(c) Try the three dilemma tales below.

What would you do?

Sharon's Tracksuit

Sharon has been saving her pocket-money for four weeks to buy a new-style tracksuit. She has seen it advertised and she is very keen to have it.

When she has bought it she calls on her friend Jane. 'Do you like it?' she asks Jane eagerly, twirling about in her new tracksuit. Jane can see that her friend thinks the tracksuit is wonderful. But to be truthful, Jane does not like it. It is purple – a colour she does not much like – and it looks too baggy. She does not want to hurt Sharon by saying what she really thinks. And she does not want to tell a lie either.

What would you do if you were Jane?

Who was right?

Julie's teacher has told the class she does not want them to bring sweets to school. The teacher says sweets are bad for their teeth and puts too much sugar into the body. One day Julie is given some money by her uncle who is staying with her family. She buys several toffee bars. Forgetting what the teacher has said, she takes three toffee bars to school. She gives one to her friend Nadia who says, 'Oh, good, we'll eat them in the playground when no one is looking.' She gives the other toffee bar to her friend Linda. But Linda gives it back and says, 'I'm going to tell the teacher, Julie. You'll get into trouble.'

Who was right – Nadia or Linda?
If Julie had offered you a toffee bar, what would you have done?

Mary's Dolphin Rubber

Mary is a quiet girl who has only one friend in class – Camilla. The two have been friends since their first days in the infant school and it seems that nothing will part them.

On Monday morning Mary brings in a very special rubber that her uncle gave her at the weekend. It is shaped like a dolphin and is very beautiful.

Camilla keeps looking at it all morning. She loves it. The more she asks to see it the more she wishes she had one of her own. When she gets home she tells her mum about it. Her mum promises to buy her one if they see it. But as hard as they both look they cannot find another dolphin rubber. Camilla is very disappointed.

Mary explains that her uncle bought the rubber in Greece, where he went for a holiday. Camilla's disappointment deepens.

On Friday, at hometime, Mary discovers that her dolphin rubber is no longer in her pencil case where she last put it. She asks Camilla if she has seen it. Camilla shakes her head, but Mary notices that she does not look her in the eye and that her friend is blushing.

Mary's heart sinks. She guesses that Camilla has taken her rubber. She is upset. But she does not want to accuse her best friend.

1 *Why doesn't Mary want to accuse her friend of taking the rubber?*
2 *What should Mary do?*

20 *What would you like to be?*

Talk expected: personal; comparative; predictive.

Objectives:
(a) to provide an opportunity for pupils to express personal preferences
(b) to make comparisons and evaluations
(c) to make predictions about themselves.

Preparation: Encourage the pupils to talk about the jobs their parents and relatives have. (Many won't know!) How many pupils already have an idea of the jobs they would like to do when adult?

Organisation:
(a) Split the class or group into twos, threes or fours.
(b) Read aloud each of the extracts on the pupil's pages. Allow the children to comment on each one if they wish.
(c) Ask the pupils to discuss the three questions in their groups.
(d) Encourage each group to report back. Does any job emerge as a favourite? What do they consider the most important, and how was the judgment made?

Extension:
(a) If numbers allow, give groups of four one of the jobs described. They have to present to the rest of the class a 'speech' which has two parts. In the first part they say why they think the rest of the class should choose this job when adult

(i.e. its advantages), and in the second they have to say why they think it is the most important job on the list.

(b) Make a class book of pictures and writing called JOBS WE WOULD LIKE TO DO WHEN WE ARE GROWN UP.

21 A problem with bullies

Talk expected: persuasive; personal.

Objectives:
(a) to explore through talk a real-life problem
(b) to evaluate several courses of action
(c) to report on personal experiences of bullying.

Preparation: Talk about the problem of bullying. Is it an issue in the school? How many pupils feel too frightened to report that they or their friends are being bullied? How can a bully be discovered and punished?

Organisation:
(a) Divide the class or group into pairs or threes.
(b) Talk about the three pictures, asking pupils to comment. If this stimulates personal experiences of bullying, encourage this so that the pupils feel there is a real purpose in discussing this problem.
(c) Ask them to consider what they would do if they were the child who was the witness.
(d) Report back. Maybe as a result of this, firm courses of action will be laid down for the class so that the same situation might be avoided for them.

Extension: Writing about bullies is a fruitful theme.

22 Make up and act a play

Talk expected: various.
Objectives:
(a) to encourage pupils to improvise a play unsupervised
(b) to develop group discussion during the play's invention
(c) to develop delivery of dialogue in performance
(d) to give an opportunity for imaginative play.

Preparation: Look out for examples of pupils spontaneously making up their own plays in the playground. Or follow up a session of improvisation in drama with this page.

Organisation:
(a) Decide how many groups you want to work on this. It could be one at a time or several simultaneously.

(b) Decide whether it is to be in the pupils' own time or whether you are going to give them lesson time.
(c) Decide whether the play is to be performed. For some this might not be appropriate.
(d) Have ready some ideas for their plays: a picture book, a theme, a short story, a well-known tale, a story poem, etc. around which the pupils can form their play. But first, give them the option of making up their own play.
(e) Give the group a realistic deadline for completion of the play, but be flexible about this.
(f) Make sure you see their work and respond positively towards it in some way.

Extension: If you are working on a theme to present to the school in assembly, pupils could act short scenes around aspects of the theme.

23 *What will you take to an island?*

Talk expected: various, i.e. persuasive, predictive, descriptive, imaginative, comparative, personal.

Objectives:
(a) to present an imaginative situation in which a range of spoken language is required
(b) to reflect on personal needs when in unfamiliar situations
(c) to provide an opportunity for group planning.

Preparation: Ask pupils whether they would like to live on a deserted island for a while with one other person. What would life be like? What would they need?

Organisation:
(a) Divide the class or group into pairs.
(b) Read the page to them. Stress that food and water are already supplied in the house.
(c) Before they begin to compile their lists, make sure they are aware that every item has to be justified.
(d) If some pairs think of more than twelve items, encourage them to continue their list and select from it that which is most important.
(e) When most pairs are ready, have a report back session in which each pair nominates the two most important items on their list. These are written on the board. From this a final selection is made by the whole class or group.
(f) Round off by asking each pair to make a list of all the things they would miss if they were on this island for a year (with no post or telephone).

24 *What can hands do?*

Talk expected: descriptive; imaginative.

Objectives:
(a) to develop descriptive and imaginative language
(b) to exercise memory.

Preparation: Talk about memory, how important it is to remember names, addresses, numbers, items on a list, instructions, directions, etc. Suggest that memory games like this one can help to exercise the ability to recall at this functional level.

Organisation:
(a) Talk about one or two things hands are good at doing.
(b) Explain the game. Have a pair of pupils demonstrate it for two or three items. Point out that remembering ten items is ambitious and that most will do well to remember five or six. Make sure that each pupil is compiling their own list which uses none of the items chosen by their partner.
(c) When it is apparent that most pairs have finished, stop the pupils and ask them to talk about their memories as revealed by this game. Were they surprised at the results? Could they improve their memories if they had lots of this sort of practice?
(d) Continue with the second idea on the pupil's page.

Extension: Encourage pupils to play variations of this game during spare moments. Subjects could be:
Books I have read
Wild animals I like best
Makes of cars I have seen
Places I have been to
Things my dad/mum are good at
Things you can do with a pot of paint.

25 Can you give directions?

Talk expected: instructive.

Objective: to develop pupils' ability to give clear geographical directions.

Preparation:
(a) Talk about the common need for giving, receiving and acting upon geographical directions. Ask pupils to give directions from one part of the school to another – this will prepare them to use the appropriate vocabulary. It may also demonstrate the need for this kind of work.
(b) Talk about the map, making sure that all the pupils can recognise its parts and labels. Compare it with their own community. In pairs, ask them to find at least six differences between the map and their neighbourhood.

Organisation:
(a) The pupils should work in pairs.
(b) One member of a pair will ask, 'How do I get to . . . from . . . if I am travelling in a car?' The other gives the appropriate directions *without* pointing at the map.
(c) When you are satisfied that the pair have used up most of the directional possibilities of the map, ask them to give each other directions to places in their own neighbourhood, saying whether they are on foot, on a cycle or in a motor vehicle.

Extension:
(a) The map could well stimulate storytelling or story writing. It provides a rich setting for this.
(b) To continue with giving directions, ask one member of a pair to give the other directions in drawing simple shapes without demonstrating, e.g. the outline of a train, a windmill, a house, a boat, a bicycle, etc. Both could be drawing, following directions given alternately.

26 Storytelling

Talk expected: narrative.

Objectives:
(a) to develop storytelling skills
(b) to increase interest in picture books
(c) to share enthusiasm for fiction.

Organisation:
(a) This activity is best done by a few individuals while the rest of the class is working on something else.
(b) Read the page with the pupil. Ask the pupil to come back to you when he/she knows the story they want to retell.
(c) If the pupil wants to retell it to you first, welcome this, but it is better not to insist on it at this stage. If the pupil made a tape you could listen to that.
(d) Ask the pupil to select two or three of her/his classmates to retell the story to. Explain to these pupils what is going to happen. Make sure the pupil is not reading the text but is retelling it in her/his own words. It can be read afterwards by the other pupils.
(e) When the group is finished, ask one or more of the pupils who heard the retelling if they would like to try this.

Extension:
(a) Once many pupils have done this – and if it has been successful – you might want to encourage a group of them to form a storytelling club, as suggested on the pupil's page.
(b) Audiences other than classmates could be used, in particular younger children in the school.

27 Can you use the telephone?

Talk expected: descriptive.

Objectives:
(a) to check on pupils' ability to use the telephone and its accessories
(b) to develop the use of descriptive language.

Preparation:
(a) Ask who has got a telephone at home. Note those who have not and make sure they are in a pair with a pupil who has.
(b) Ask for a count of those who feel confident in using a telephone. How many of them are forbidden to use the telephone without permission from their parents? Do they know why?
(c) Ask them to discuss in pairs why they think it is important that children of their age learn to use the telephone, and then to report back.

Organisation:
(a) The page has two sets of tasks. Explain the first one to the pupils and let them work in pairs on it. At a convenient point call a halt to the discussion and go through the questions as a class.
(b) The second part – Imaginary Telephone Conversations – contains suggestions for descriptive and imaginative talk. If you have ex-British Telecom receivers or toy telephones for this, all the better. Encourage the pupil receiving the conversation to ask plenty of relevant questions.

Extension: Some pupils could make a picture sequence chart explaining how to use a public telephone (photographs could be used instead of drawings). This could be used to inform other classes and displayed in school as an aide-mémoire.

28 What should Gail do?

Talk expected: persuasive; comparative.

Objectives:
(a) to consider several alternative outcomes of a problem
(b) to use argument to persuade others
(c) to consider consequences of actions.

Organisation:
(a) Split the class or group into pairs or threes.
(b) Talk about the situation presented on the pupil's page. Ask pupils to talk about the seven alternatives in turn, thinking about the good and bad things in each. Then ask them to put them in the order they think best.
(c) Record the results on the board, giving a tick for each number voted for by each pupil. Do you agree with the most popular outcome?

29 What happens next?

Talk expected: narrative; predictive.

Objectives: to develop storytelling and prediction.

Preparation: To lead into the story, talk about the experience of arriving home early (like Daniel) and wanting to do something to please the rest of the household when they arrive. Has anyone in the group or class been in this situation?

Organisation:
(a) Divide the class or group into pairs or threes.
(b) Read *all* the story through with the pupils first – it will give them a secure framework in which to work. Talk about the kind of boy Daniel is.
(c) Explain the nature of the task. Ask them to have a go at the first part.
(d) After five or ten minutes, stop the discussion and invite reporting back. Make a list on the board of the alternatives given. Which are the best and why? In the process, emphasise the need for detail to make the episode in the story more vivid and interesting – it is the detail which is often lacking in this sort of work. Stress that in the second episode you are looking for much more detail.
(e) After the next two episodes, repeat the reporting back process if you think this would be of value.

Extension:
(a) Having talked about Daniel and his situation, the pupils might like to write or act stories about him.
(b) Occasionally, when reading a short story or fable to the pupils, you could ask them to predict what might happen next.

30 Aesop's Fables – what's the moral?

Talk expected: persuasive; interpretative.

Objectives:
(a) to provide a stimulus for persuasive and interpretative language
(b) to encourage pupils to give reasoned responses
(c) to develop an interest in the fable form
(d) to help pupils focus on the main idea or theme of a story.

Preparation: Find a good collection of Aesop's fables at the right level and read some of them to the pupils, choosing those which have a stated moral. Write the morals on the board *before* the stories are read, and after the reading ask the class or group to select from the list on the board the most appropriate moral for the story. This will help pupils to understand the nature of a fable's moral.

Organisation:
(a) Divide the class or group into twos, threes or fours.
(b) Ask each group to read each fable and find the best moral. Make sure they consider each alternative and have a good reason for the one they have chosen.
(c) Ask some groups to report back.

Extension:
(a) A few of the more able pupils might like to write their own fables. Most fables feature animals as the main characters. To help these children, you could provide them with some morals – perhaps taken from other fables – around which they can build their own fables.
(b) The rest of the pupils could illustrate a short fable (for this you would need plenty of copies of different fables), writing the story in their own words to accompany their picture.

31 If I ruled the world . . .

Talk expected: persuasive; personal; comparative.

Objectives:
(a) to stimulate pupils to share their views of the world
(b) to consider and compare alternative viewpoints
(c) to argue for and against changes.

Preparation: Open up the theme by saying that at one time or another most of us have dreamed of the changes we would make if we ruled the world.

Organisation:
(a) Divide the class or group into pairs or threes.
(b) Read aloud Amanda's piece on the pupil's page. (It comes from *Dear World*, edited by H. & R. Exley, Exley Publications. This book contains an interesting and international collection of children's views about the world.)
(c) Ask groups to make a list of things they agree with in the list and another one for those they disagree with.
(d) Circulate, asking groups to justify the placing of some of the items in their two lists.
(e) Ask some groups to report back by reading out one or two items from each list, giving reasons for their views.
(f) Groups can then draw up a list of changes they would make if they ruled the world. There could be reporting back on some of these too. Invite other groups to challenge any of these changes, and don't be afraid to question any of them yourself, if some appear bizarre.

Extension:
(a) The lists could be copied and displayed with pictures or made into a large illustrated class book.
(b) This would make an interesting theme for a class assembly.

32 Can you tell a well-known story?

Talk expected: narrative.

Objectives:
(a) to develop storytelling
(b) to ensure that pupils know some of the traditional tales.

Preparation:
(a) Talk to the pupils about the oral tradition – about how stories were once told rather than read and that many of the stories they know began like this. Ask the pupils which stories they like best – how many can retell these stories?
(b) Have ready some versions of the traditional tales listed on the pupil's page in case some children are not familiar with these stories.

Organisation:

(a) Groups can be between three and five.

(b) Read the instructions on the pupil's page and make sure they are understood. Stress that help can be given by others to the pupil retelling the story.

(c) Circulate and listen to some of the stories. Listen particularly for detail, accuracy, sequence and liveliness of language. Make suggestions for improvements when appropriate, but otherwise try not to interrupt the flow. Some pupils will be very self-conscious about this activity and will need considerable encouragement; they may be better off in pairs.

Extension:

(a) Take a vote on which story of the five they prefer. Ask for reasons.

(b) Some groups might want to act one of the stories to show the infant children.

33 What's it like?

Talk expected: imaginative; descriptive; explanatory.

Objectives:

(a) to stimulate pupils to consider and explain similes

(b) to help pupils think imaginatively

(c) to give opportunities for descriptive language.

Preparation:

(a) Make sure you have at least 22 slips of paper for each pair of pupils doing this activity, and another pile of spare slips for follow-up work.

(b) Talk about the use of similes to explain what things are *like*.

Organisation:

(a) Divide the class or group into pairs.

(b) Explain what is required. Demonstrate the first one to give an idea of how to match stem with simile.

(c) When the pupils begin to match up their stems and similes, circulate and ask them to justify some of their matches: 'Why is that a good simile?'

The ones I have in mind are:

A tortoise is like a walking hut.

A spider is like a mop with only eight hairs.

A giraffe is like a walking tree with two leaves.

A lion is like a sandy rug with a giant roar.

A sheep is like a large walking wig.

A hawk is like a kite without a string.

An elephant is like a loose pipe fixed to a big tank.

A monkey is like a naughty child in a fur coat.

A caterpillar is like a wriggly green chippolata.

A hippopotamus is like a large boulder on legs.

A pig is like a huge hairy pink balloon.

Extension:

(a) Some pupils might like to have a go at writing their own stems and similes for matching, perhaps concentrating on insects.

(b) Each of the matchings above would make a good subject for a cartoon.

34 Who do you agree with?

Talk expected: persuasive; personal.

Objectives:
(a) to discuss several viewpoints
(b) to help pupils reflect on characters in fiction.

Preparation: Talk to the pupils about their families' rules about sweets. Are sweets ever given as a reward for good behaviour? What reasons would there be for withholding sweets from children?

Organisation:
(a) Split the class or group into twos, threes or fours.
(b) Encourage each pupil to follow the story as you read it aloud.
(c) Ask·a group of pupils to read out the comments made at the end of the story. Avoid giving your own views at this stage. Each group has to discuss the two questions posed after these comments as well as the comments themselves.
(d) While the groups are discussing the questions and comments, draw columns on the board, each labelled with one of the names of the children: Nera, Raymond, Opu, Emma and Ashok. The final one is left clear for your pupils' alternative views.
(e) Ask groups to report back. Record agreement with the five children's views by putting a tick in the appropriate column; alternative views can be written in the sixth column. Has any pattern emerged?

Extension:
(a) To record their own view of eating sweets, the pupils could write a short piece entitled: 'What I Think About Eating Sweets'.
(b) You could link this with a project on dental health.

35 Can you explain how to do something?

Talk expected: instructive; descriptive.

Objective:
(a) to give pupils the opportunity to explain a process in a clear sequence to another child
(b) to enhance listening and memory
(c) to develop the ability to repeat what one has been told.

Preparation:
(a) Explain that we use spoken language a lot to pass on knowledge and skills. The clearer the language the easier for the other person to understand. All of us have got something to teach – but how good are we at teaching it? These three activities will help test and improve pupils' ability to pass on knowledge effectively.
(b) Make sure you have a book or card – pictorial as well as verbal – which explains how to make pancakes and mend a puncture. You may have to make some workcards yourself.

Organisation:
(a) Decide how many pairs will be working on this at any one time.
(b) Call up the 'teachers' in the pairs and explain what is required. Give them the means to discover or check how to make pancakes and mend a puncture.
(c) When these pupils think they know one of the two processes, get them to repeat it to you so that you can check its accuracy. Then send them back to their partners to pass on the knowledge.
(d) If you wish, you can check whether the partner has fully understood what the first pupil said.
(e) When both processes are explained – or you may wish to restrict it to one per pair – move on to the third task, which is explaining how to play a game.

Extension:
(a) It would, of course, be much more meaningful if the pairs could then go on to make pancakes and mend a puncture, but this may raise practical problems.
(b) Each pupil could be set a 'teaching task' where they have to pass on some practical knowledge to a partner. A chart could be made and displayed on the wall, showing the pupil's name, type of knowledge being passed on, to whom, and the date it happened.

The SPOKEN WORD Project

Book 2: Talk it Over

(for Middle Junior pupils)

1 Golden Rules for talking in groups

This page appears in all three course books. Please refer to the notes for Book 1 (p. 18).

2 To talk about before you start

Talk expected: persuasive; predictive; comparative.

Objectives:
(a) to compare the different functions of the four main forms of verbal communication
(b) to give opportunities for persuasive talk
(c) to focus on the role of talk in everyday situations.

Preparation: It may help to refer to the same section in Book 1 to open up this discussion. Otherwise talk about the different purposes of talking, listening, reading and writing in everyday life.

Organisation:
(a) Divide the class into pairs or threes.
(b) Ask the groups to think of three purposes each for reading, writing, talking and listening. Record the best of these on the board under the appropriate headings.
(c) Ask the groups which of the four they think they will need most in their lives, giving reasons.
(d) Report back. Take a vote from each pupil. Which emerges as the favourite?
(e) Ask groups to consider the list of situations given on the pupil's page. This can be done collectively if you prefer. Again, record their votes. It will be seen that several of the situations use more than one form of verbal communication to equal effect.
(f) Round off this discussion by considering the final question on the pupil's page. Again, this is better done in pairs or threes, with some reporting back.

Extension: Look at the two extension ideas for this activity in Book 1 (p. 19). If they have not already been done by the children, you could use them.

3 Whose side are you on?

Talk expected: persuasive; predictive; narrative.

Objectives:
(a) to reflect upon the contrasting viewpoints of two fictional characters
(b) to argue persuasively
(c) to raise the issue of sexism in stories and in life
(d) to provide opportunities for imaginative prediction.

Preparation: Talk about the traditional role of princesses in fairy tales, their general submissiveness, decorativeness, lack of power, vulnerability, etc. Point out

46

that some stories, including modern fairy stories, can be different. Judy Corbalis's collection, of which this is the opening pages, is a good example of the traditional fairy tale turned on its head.

Organisation:
(a) Divide the class or group into threes. Make sure there is a competent reader in each group.
(b) Either read the story aloud to the pupils, or let them read it themselves.
(c) Appoint a narrator (i.e. the best reader) for each group. Let the group decide who plays the king (and page) and who plays the princess. The narrator should then read the text aloud, the others joining in when appropriate.
(d) Encourage the groups to discuss the first three questions. Give them plenty of time for this and have a full reporting back session.
(e) Do the same with point 4 on the pupil's page.
(f) If you have a copy of the book of stories, read them the rest of this story and compare the author's plot with some of those suggested by the groups.

Extension:
(a) Use the story – and some of the others in Judy Corbalis's book if you have it – for improvised drama.
(b) Some of the more able writers may wish to write a short play about Princess Ermyntrude, based on what happened to her in the story.
(c) Find some more non-sexist fairy stories, e.g. Jay Williams, *The Practical Princess*, Macmillan; James Riordan, *The Woman in the Moon*, Hutchinson; and Alison Lurie, *Clever Gretchen and Other Forgotten Heroines*, Heinemann. Read some of them to the class over the next few weeks.
(d) See Book 3, Unit 14 for more work on the theme of sexism.

4 *Can you exaggerate?*

Talk expected: narrative; descriptive.

Objectives: to give opportunities for pupils to develop descriptive and narrative language in a humorous way.

Preparation: Introduce the word 'exaggeration' by writing it on the board and giving examples of what it means so that the pupils are familiar with the concept. Point out that exaggerations form part of our common speech and are used to give emphasis; for example, we say 'I'm freezing' when we mean we are cold, or 'It was as hard as nails' when referring, perhaps, to a stale cake. Exaggerations, by making everything larger than life, can form the basis for comic descriptions and stories.

Organisation:
(a) Arrange the pupils into pairs or small groups.
(b) Read the pupil's page with them. Talk about the character of Ebenezer.
(c) Listen in to the discussions. Invite a few individuals to report back with their exaggerations if you wish.
(d) If this proves successful, try out with the whole class or a group the first idea for an Ebenezer story: *The Day Ebenezer Took His Driving Test*. Jot down the pupils' ideas for it so that you can retell it to them later; stress that the story

should be as exaggerated as possible.
(e) Let the pairs or small groups choose one of the other three ideas to work on. Pick out any promising pairs or groups to record their stories later.

Extension: Some pupils may well want to write their stories. If the character of Ebenezer 'takes off' – as it will in some classes – the pupils could invent further stories in talk, writing, cartoons and drama, and make little books based on him.

5 Can you plan a picture book?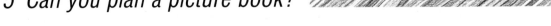

Talk expected: descriptive; explanatory.

Objectives:
(a) to help pupils plan and research a given topic
(b) to consider its visual presentation
(c) to make books or concertina cards
(d) to communicate in verbal as well as visual terms what has been learned.

Preparation:
(a) It is essential that you have reference books at the right level to explain the seven processes listed on the pupil's page.
(b) It would also help if you had a few wordless picture books to show. There is a series of these by Ginn & Co Ltd called *First Nature Watch* which provide models for this activity.
(c) Talk about the value of transmitting knowledge visually to young children who, because of deafness, have difficulty with oral information.

Organisation:
(a) Divide the class or group into twos, threes or fours, and give each group one of the processes listed, together with appropriate reference books.
(b) Explain the nature of the task. The first stage is the research and planning. Suggest that the group limit their picture book to no more than ten pages. Ask them to present to you, after their research and discussion, a list of titles in the right sequence for the pictures. Check them for accuracy. Ask the group to retell to you the process, then to repeat it to another group.
(c) Let the groups make their picture books, sharing the tasks.
(d) Ask each group to read and talk about their book with a group of younger children.
(e) Make a display of these books for others to read.

6 What would you choose?

Talk expected: persuasive; comparative.

Preparation: Introduce the topic by talking about how a school is funded, who makes the important decisions regarding its facilities, and about the role of the governors.

(a) Groups of three or four would be best for this, to share a range of views.
(b) Briefly talk about the value to a school of each of the items listed on the pupil's page. Explain the problem of choice facing the governors and ask the pupils to consider the problem. Reasons for choosing and rejecting are, of course, essential.
(c) Report back, questioning and making pupils elaborate on their responses. Make a list of the items on the board and mark votes for each from individual pupils.
(d) Ask if the group can come up with another important item the money could be spent on.
(e) What would they spend £20,000 on in their own school?

7 Which rules would you have?

Talk expected: persuasive.

Objectives:
(a) to develop persuasive argument in groups
(b) to consider the rules governing pupils' behaviour at school.

Preparation: Talk about the rules governing the behaviour of the pupils in your school, both the spoken and unspoken rules, and find out whether the pupils (1) are aware of the rules, (2) understand the reasons for them, and (3) agree with all of them.

Organisation:
(a) The pupils should be in groups of three or four.
(b) Read aloud the two sets of rules while the pupils follow on the page.
(c) Make sure they understand that there are two separate tasks. Firstly, they have to come to a group agreement on which *set* of rules they prefer and why, regardless of whether some of the individual rules within the set are not to their liking. Secondly, which individual rules would they select from both lists to make up a third one? The group will need a scribe to record their conclusions.
(d) Report back. Firstly, go through each of the rules in Class A's list, inviting arguments for and against each. Then take a count of which groups favour this list overall. Secondly, do the same with Class B's list.
(e) Now ask the groups to tell you which rules they prefer from both lists. You can record this in two columns – for Class A and Class B – on the board, giving a tick for each rule number supported. At the end of this you will have a picture of which rules your class most favour.
(f) Finally, ask the pupils to suggest additional rules they think are necessary to the smooth running of their school. Which of these rules would find favour ˙ with you and other staff and pupils?

Extension:
(a) A group of pupils could draw up a list of rules for the smooth running of their own class or base. These could then be presented to the rest of the class for their comment and final approval (assuming, of course, that you find them sensible!).

(b) The pupils could try to record what they think are the spoken and unspoken rules governing their behaviour at home.

8 Can you solve these problems?

Talk expected: descriptive; explanatory; narrative.

Objectives:
(a) to present practical problems for a range of possible solutions
(b) in the process of problem-solving, to elicit descriptive, explanatory and narrative language.

Preparation: You could read a few animal fables to the pupils – ones which include problems – to put them in the mood for this activity.

Organisation:
(a) Split the class or group into pairs or threes.
(b) Explain that the animals in the pictures can talk, as in fables. Otherwise they are still limited by their physical capabilities. You are looking for imaginative as well as practical solutions.
(c) Ask the pupils to do the first one. After five or ten minutes have a report back session so that each group has a good idea thereafter of what to do. You could list in note form on the board the different solutions suggested, then ask the class to vote on the one they find most practical and the one they find most inventive and interesting.
(d) The pupils could then do the next three problems. You could have them report back after each one but this could break up the flow of discussion; so it might be better to have just one reporting back session at the end.

Extension: Can the pupils think up their own animal problems in picture form for others to try and solve?

9 What does it mean?

Talk expected: interpretative.

Objectives:
(a) to give opportunities for interpretative discussion
(b) to encourage pupils to look at familiar things afresh.

Preparation: Talk with the class or group about a Martian's-eye view of our world; how everything would look strange to it because the reasons for actions and objects would not be apparent and because everyday language would be strange or deficient. What would this Martian write on a postcard to send back home?

Organisation:
(a) Split the class into pairs or threes.
(b) Ask them to discuss the meaning of the first postcard – or do it all together –

and then share interpretations.
(c) Groups should then discuss each postcard, making notes if they wish on the various interpretations possible. The texts are deliberately ambiguous to allow for several different meanings. The meanings the author had in mind follow, but any meaning, well-argued by the pupils will be equally valid.

Postcard 1: children go to school, are let out to play on playgrounds and paths, hold hands with each other or fight using fists.

Postcard 2: children watch television, read, get in adults' way, sleep.

Postcard 3: adults drive cars, throw darts, fish, live in houses.

Postcard 4: adults hug each other, use the telephone, do gardening, are buried when dead.

(d) Once these cards have been discussed, ask the pupils to have a go at writing one or two Martian postcards similar to these. Write the results on real postcards and display them on a pinboard around a big painting of a Martian. You will then have a display to stimulate more discussion.

10 What would you do?

Talk expected: persuasive; imaginative; predictive.

Objectives:
(a) to develop listening by following a visual sequence that illustrates a story being heard
(b) to consider a real-life problem
(c) to give opportunities to express opinions
(d) to encourage imaginative identification with characters in stories.

Preparation: Talk with the pupils about the problems a newcomer might have in adjusting to a new group of children, and about friendship – special friends, acquaintances, relating to friends of friends, etc.

Organisation:
(a) Split the class or group into pairs or threes.
(b) Make sure each can follow the picture sequence.
(c) Read the story below aloud.
(d) Ask groups to discuss the first question on their page. Report back on this. Make a note of some of their responses on the board and see if any consensus emerges as to what Sheila should do.
(e) The group should then discuss the next two questions and report back.

Extension: Friendship – and its lack – is a fruitful theme for a mini-project, to be explored in stories, drama and literature.

Anna and Sheila

A new girl, Anna, comes to school and she is put next to Sheila. At first Anna is very quiet, talks almost in whispers and seems very shy. Sheila decides to help Anna as much as she can and within a week they are firm friends.

Sheila has many friends. She tries to make them friends of Anna too. But, strangely, this does not work. Anna is too shy with them and they say she is a bit odd, a bit stuck up.

'Why don't you try harder to make friends?' Sheila asks more than once. Anna usually shakes her head. 'One's enough,' she is fond of saying.

Things get worse. Sheila's friends begin to call Anna names and they tease her cruelly. When Sheila sticks up for Anna they say she must be a fool.

One day Sheila's friends come to her and say, 'If you stay friendly with that Anna we shan't be friends with you any more.' Sheila protests, but they won't change their minds.

Sheila knows that if she stops being Anna's friend then Anna will be lonely. 'But it's her fault,' Sheila says to herself. 'Oh, what shall I do?'

11 What should James do?

Talk expected: persuasive; comparative; predictive.

Objectives: to stimulate pupils to discuss a range of different solutions to a problem, weighing the merits and consequences of each.

Organisation:
(a) Divide the class or group into pairs, threes or fours.
(b) Make sure each group can follow the picture sequence as you read aloud the story below.
(c) Ask the groups to consider in turn each of the first six questions listed on their page. You could ask them to list the good and bad points of each.
(d) Have a reporting back session in which arguments for and against each point are raised.
(e) Consider question 7. Are any other solutions forthcoming?
(f) Finally, take a vote, allowing each individual a separate vote.

James and Mr Fraser

Mr Fraser lived on his own. He was retired, and what he liked above all else was peace and quiet. If there were children playing outside his house, out he would go and shoo them away with rough, loud words. When *he* had been a boy more than half a century ago he had played outside people's houses and could never understand why adults got so upset about the noise – but he had forgotten that.

James lived in a house roughly at right-angles to Mr Fraser's. He had been shooed away many times for making too much noise and he was a bit afraid of Mr Fraser. But he also felt a little sorry for the old man – living alone and being old, who wouldn't be grumpy?

One day James was at his bedroom window. He saw Mr Fraser set off down the road carrying a shopping bag.

James left the window for a few minutes, and when he looked out of it again he saw two girls knocking at Mr Fraser's door. He recognised the girls. They went to his school, but he was not friends with them. In fact, one of them had once pinched his best rubber and the teacher had refused to believe she took it. So James scowled when he saw the two girls at Mr Fraser's door.

He wondered what they wanted. He became more curious when he saw them glance up and down the street and then slip quickly round to the back of Mr Fraser's house. What were they up to? He ran into his parents' bedroom. From there he could see into Mr Fraser's back garden. The girls were nowhere to be seen. Which meant only one thing – they had entered Mr Fraser's house.

That took some nerve, thought James. If Mr Fraser caught them he would march them straight down to the police station. But what were they up to? Were they about to burgle the old man?

James looked back up the street and saw Mr Fraser returning, carrying a heavy shopping bag and moving slowly as if he were tired.

James froze, unable to decide what to do. What should he do?

Talk about each of the seven points on the pupil's page before deciding what James should do.

12 What a riddle!

Talk expected: interpretative.

Objectives:
(a) to stimulate interpretative discussion in which reference to details is important
(b) to introduce the riddle form.

Preparation: The riddles on the pupil's page are purposely demanding in order to stimulate discussion. If they had been too easy, discussion would have ended as soon as the answer had been guessed. So, to introduce the riddle form it is a good idea to find some easier riddles and try them out on the pupils. This will set the context and give them the confidence to tackle the riddles on the page. You will find four easier riddles in Book 1 of this course (see p. 23).

Organisation:
(a) Divide the class or group into pairs.
(b) Read aloud the three riddles. Read each one twice, making sure that they are being followed by the pupils. Point out that they are not easy and that it will be surprising if all three are solved by any one pair. Also, make sure that the pupils understand that any answer must match *all* the clues in the riddle, not just some. Insist, too, that possible answers are not called out at this stage but noted in secret.
(c) If you have a significant number of poor readers in class, for whom these riddles will be too hard, give them some easier ones to discuss.
(d) Have a reporting back session. Accept more than one answer to the same riddle if they prove valid.
(e) The answers the author had in mind are as follows: Riddle 1: dust, Riddle 2: a ball point pen, Riddle 3: a mirror. Discuss each answer in the light of each detail given in the riddles.

Extension: If this proves popular with some pupils, ask them to make a book of riddles or a display of them, some of which they have collected, some which they have written themselves.

13 Can you peer into the future?

Talk expected: imaginative; descriptive; narrative.

Objective: to stimulate imaginative description.

Preparation: Talk about the claims some people make that they can see into the future. The pupils will probably be familiar with the idea of the crystal ball as a tool for prophecy. What you will need to guard against with this activity is the tendency for some pupils not to take it seriously, in the spirit intended. It will help in this regard if you present it in the context of fantasy – as an important element in a science-fiction story, perhaps, or a story containing wizards, etc. Some of the pupils will be familiar with this kind of story through popular publications such as Puffin's *Fighting Fantasy Gamebooks* as well as through comics. Ask pupils to imagine who once owned the box and why it was buried.

Organisation:
(a) Divide the class or group into threes or fours.
(b) Insist on a few minutes absolute quiet while each pupil tries to create an image of something in the future which he or she can describe to the others.
(c) Let every pupil describe to their group what they saw and what they think it means or shows.
(d) Ask groups to list what each pupil imagined, writing a descriptive sentence or two for each. These could then be put in order of importance by the group.
(e) Ask individuals to report back. You could list on the board some of the things imagined and then discuss these in terms of their likelihood, their negative or positive elements, whether they already exist in some form today, etc.

Extension:
(a) Ask each pupil to draw inside a crystal ball (i.e. a circle) what they imagined. Display these in a book or on a pinboard entitled 'Our Visions of the Future'.
(b) Encourage the pupils to write stories in which they are transported to the future.

14 Can you write a radio play?

Talk expected: narrative; imaginative.

Objectives:
(a) to stimulate group collaborative discussion
(b) to focus on ways of rendering dialogue in writing
(c) to choose a story and turn it into a playscript
(d) to develop 'performance skills' using speech alone.

Preparation:
(a) Playwriting is something that many older juniors find stimulating and absorbing. It is, however, a relatively neglected form of writing in the junior school, and it is therefore quite likely that your pupils will never have attempted the writing of a playscript. If this is so, they will need to be sure

about how to lay out the words of a script on the page. The most effective way of introducing this is to give them a playscript – there are many of them now on the market for group reading in the primary school – to read through together. If you do this, the context is set and the method made familiar. However, if playscripts are not available you can show the layout of a script by writing an example of it on the board, perhaps adapting for this purpose the beginning of a well-known story or the opening pages of a picture book. The script on the pupil's page will help with this. Once you are confident that the pupils know how to read and write a playscript (in theory at least), proceed.

(b) Collect together a sufficient number of picture books, short stories and fables which you judge to be suitable for the pupils to adapt into playscripts. Look for stories that:
    (1) are not too long
    (2) do not have a complicated plot or plots
    (3) have only a handful of main characters
    (4) do not have too many scene changes.

Organisation:

(a) Read to the pupils the extract from *Zeralda's Ogre* by Tomi Ungerer, making sure the pupils are following it. Explain that this has been transformed into the script on the pupil's page, then read that aloud. Ask for volunteers to take the parts of the Ogre, Boy, the father and Zeralda, then re-read the script aloud. Stress that most of the story is told *through dialogue*. (Recourse to a narrator figure is possible but should be used sparingly.)

(b) Divide the class or group into pairs, threes, fours (mixed ability groups?). Give each group a few of the books you have chosen and ask the pupils to spend some time considering which they would like to adapt. Ask them to give reasons for their final choice.

(c) Let them have a go at adapting the first page or so. Some pupils will find this no trouble, others will need considerable help in breaking away from the prose narrative they have been used to. The writing task should be shared, the book in which they are writing being passed from pupil to pupil for each new speaker. It is best *not* to insist that each pupil is responsible for one of the character's words, as in practice this seldom works. Rough drafting is natural for this activity and you will find the pupils turning to it readily. Much discussion on how the story should proceed, what to cut out and what the characters say will be evident, and the collaborative discussion is often intense.

(d) Several quite lengthy writing sessions will be needed to complete the scripts, and these sessions should be kept close together – successive days are best.

(e) As the groups finish writing their rough drafts, read them aloud with the groups. Suggest changes where necessary. The script can then be copied out, everyone in the group sharing this task.

(f) The plays should then be rehearsed, recorded on tape and then played to an audience.

15 What do these proverbs mean?

Talk expected: interpretative; persuasive; explanatory.

Objectives:
(a) to interpret well-known proverbs and relate them to situations in everyday life
(b) to persuade others that one's interpretation is the best.

Preparation: Talk about proverbs, how they are used mainly in speech to sum up a situation and as a basic rule of thumb. As illustrations, you could read some of the proverbs in Book 1 of this course (p. 25). Many of them will be familiar to the pupils. However, such familiarity often leads, in young children, to puzzlement rather than understanding, so this activity will bring a welcome clarification to many.

Organisation:
(a) Divide the class or group into pairs, threes or fours.
(b) Do the first two proverbs with the whole group or class, giving one or two illustrations of what the proverbs would mean in everyday situations.
(c) Ask the groups to do the next three proverbs, making use of the clues given. They should report back and share their understanding.
(d) Repeat for the last three proverbs.
(e) Do the pupils know any other proverbs? If so, discuss them.

Extension: Proverbs can make good subjects for cartoons. Each pupil takes a proverb and draws a literal rendering of it. Display these pictures on a pinboard or in a large class book and ask pupils to guess which proverb is illustrated.

16 Who should be left behind?

Talk expected: persuasive; imaginative.

Objectives:
(a) to argue persuasively for a point of view
(b) to argue persuasively against other points of view.

Preparation: Read the opening three paragraphs to the whole class or group and discuss the situation presented.

Organisation:
(a) Divide the class into groups so that there are, if possible, eight groups in all.
(b) Give each group one of the occupations to argue for. Talk briefly to the whole class about the duties of each occupation and their value to society.
(c) Ask groups to compile a list of reasons why their occupation is the most important. They should then discuss each of the other occupations to try and find reasons why these jobs are less important than the one the group is championing. It would help if the group kept notes.
(d) Have a reporting back session. For each occupation, record on a separate sheet of paper (large enough to be seen by all the pupils) the pros and cons of each job as they are listed by the groups. Display these side by side so that you have

eight charts at the end of the reporting back. After each group has reported back, encourage other groups to challenge what has been said; these challenges could also be recorded on the charts if they cannot be refuted.

(e) Alternative: divide class into groups of eight. Each group ranks occupations in order of importance. Compare results.

Extension: If this activity proves popular it could be repeated with a different set of occupations.

17 Can you solve this problem?

Talk expected: imaginative; explanatory; descriptive.

Objective: to stimulate problem-solving discussion.

Organisation:
(a) Divide the class or group into pairs, threes or fours.
(b) Make sure each pupil can follow the picture sequence as you read the first part of the story below.
(c) Encourage pupils to think of at least one solution to the crow's problem.
(d) Have a reporting back session. List the different answers on the board. Which do the pupils like best?
(e) Read the second half of the story. Did any pupil use the same idea? Is it the best of all those suggested?

The Clever Crow *Part One*

There was a drought and the dusty black crow, perched on the branch of a parched tree, was worried. He had searched all morning for water, but now there were only dry river beds and fields of caked mud where the lakes used to be. He was tired, too, much too tired to flap miles up country where water might still be flowing.

Then he caught sight of an old pitcher standing in the shade of a cottage. There was just hope, he thought, swooping down. Imagine the quickening of his heart when he saw, there in the bottom of the pitcher, the shimmer of water.

But how was he to get at the water? He poked in his yellow beak, then his dusty head, then his outstretched neck, and even half his body, but he could not reach that precious water. The pitcher was deep, the water low.

For a few minutes the crow stamped about in frustration, glaring at the pitcher. Then he huddled in despair. He knew that if he had been able to lean a couple of inches deeper he might have reached the water – but he would have overbalanced before then. Once inside the pitcher he would have been trapped, or – just as bad – might have tipped the pitcher up and lost the water. He thought to himself, 'How can I reach the water?'

Part Two

As the crow huddled, feeling more thirsty than ever, his gaze rested on a nice smooth pebble. It reminded him of a game he used to play with his brothers and sisters before they had all flown far from their parents. Who could put the most pebbles in an old tin can? Sometimes, on mornings after that game there was rain from the night glistening on the pebbles.

He lifted a pebble with his beak and dropped it into the pitcher. It made a satisfying plop. One by one he dropped pebbles in. The sound gradually changed to a clink and then a splash. Every now and then the crow paused and peered into the pitcher and saw to his satisfaction that the level of the water was rising.

The moment came, that delicious longed-for moment, when his weary, parched, dusty beak touched water. He sipped it carefully, sip after sip, and although it tasted a little stale, it seemed the finest drink he'd ever had.

18 Talking in dialect

Objectives:
(a) to introduce pupils to the idea that dialect can be written down
(b) to raise the whole subject of dialect
(c) to give pupils practice in reading aloud as a performance art.

Preparation: Talk about the prevalence of dialect and its difference from Standard English. Mention indigenous dialects – such as the Somerset one used in the story on the pupil's page – and ones which have been brought in from other countries such as India, the West Indies, etc. Is any dialect spoken by yourself or by the pupils? If so, have a go at recording it phonetically on the board to show the pupils that attempts can be made to write it down.

Organisation:
(a) This is probably best done by fluent readers in small groups rather than the whole or a large part of the class, especially as a tape-recorder will be needed for each group.
(b) Read aloud to the group the beginning of the story, so that they get the idea. Point out how the dialect spellings give vital clues to pronunciation (if the pupils are from Somerset, of course, they will find this easier). Tell the pupils that the story goes on to relate how a giant man-eating worm is finally cut in half by a woodman.
(c) Let the pupils choose themselves whether they read it aloud together or take it in turns to read parts. When they feel ready they can have a go at taping it in a quiet place.
(d) The group can then go on to do numbers 2–4 on their page – unless, of course, you feel that they have already worked hard enough on this story and to do more would be asking too much.

Extension: You could explore dialect poems and stories further. Try and get hold of the following collections, all of which have some dialect material in them:
Hamilton, Virginia: *The People Could Fly*, Walker Books, 1985, a collection of black American folktales.
O'Brien, Edna: *Tales for the Telling*, Pavilion/Michael Joseph, 1986, Irish folktales, two of which are in dialect.
Also: two volumes of multicultural poetry edited by Morag Styles and published by Cambridge University Press: *I Like That Stuff* and *You'll Love This Stuff*.

19 Can you continue the story?

Talk expected: narrative; predictive.

Objective: to provide starting points for the invention of stories and to give practice in storytelling.

Organisation:
(a) Divide the class or group into pairs or threes.
(b) Read aloud the opening paragraph on the pupil's page.
(c) Decide whether you want to give the groups a choice of the two story starters, or whether you want them all to work on the same one at the same time. If the former, read aloud both starters. If the latter, read aloud the one you want them to start with.
(d) Ask for a few opening suggestions about what could happen next in the stories and jot these on the board to act as prompts for those groups whose invention might be faltering.
(e) Circulate, making suggestions to those groups who are not finding this activity easy.
(f) It may not be appropriate to have a reporting back session, but offer it to those groups or individuals who feel confident enough to retell their story to the whole class.

Extension:
(a) Some pupils may wish to record their stories on tape or in writing.
(b) You could use some of the stories resulting from this session in improvised drama.
(c) If this activity seems promising, look for other story starters – such as the beginnings of folk and fairy tales, picture books and short stories – to repeat it.

20 Compare these buildings

Talk expected: comparative; descriptive.

Objectives:
(a) to stimulate descriptive and comparative talk
(b) to sharpen perception
(c) to exercise memory.

Preparation: Get the pupils to describe some buildings they know well. Talk about how an architect decides on the look of the building and how fashions change in architecture as time passes. Also, how the function of buildings will decide their appearance. The two pictures on the pupil's page exemplify these points.

Organisation:
(a) The class or group should be in pairs.
(b) Explain what is required, stressing that this activity tests their perception and their memory, and that all differences spotted have to be spoken and repeated to the partner.

(c) Circulate and listen to the pairs when they have reached five differences each. Encourage them to see how many more they can remember.
(d) Report back, listing all the differences in two columns on the board, using information supplied by the pupils.

Extension: If this activity proves popular it could be repeated using pairs of pictures which you or the pupils have found.

21 Can you give directions?

Talk expected: instructive.

Objective: to give pupils practice in giving accurate geographical directions.

Preparation: Discuss the need to be able to give accurate geographical directions. Ask one or two pupils to give directions from one place in the school to another, or in the immediate locality. Also, the pupils could do Unit 25 in Book 1 (if it has not already been done) which gives them the support of a map.

Organisation:
(a) The pupils should be in pairs.
(b) Read the rules aloud while the pupils follow them. Explain the rules.
(c) Circulate while the pupils play, to see that the rules are being applied.

22 Can you fill in the missing parts?

Talk expected: descriptive; imaginative; narrative.

Objectives:
(a) to give practice in imaginative description and storytelling
(b) to work cooperatively on creating a story.

Preparation: To create a context and vocabulary for this activity, it would help if you read to the class or group short stories about pirates, preferably comic ones. The *Captain Pugwash* picture books by John Ryan (Picture Puffin) are ideal. Also, Rose Impey's *Who's a Clever Girl, Then?* (Banana Books, Heinemann), which gave the general idea for this activity. Talk to the pupils about their notions of storybook pirates (many of them will be familiar with Sheila McCulloch's *Tim and the Pirates* series).

Organisation:
(a) This activity is best done in threes or fours.
(b) Explain that parts of the story are missing and it is the group's job to fill them in with as much interesting detail as they can.
(c) Have a trial run, during which the groups say what Millie looks like, what her cat looks like and how it lost its ear. Then stop and have some reporting back on this. Emphasise at this point the need for colourful detail and interesting actions. Then let the groups continue.

(d) Circulate, listening in and suggesting ideas where necessary.
(e) Have a reporting back session. Keep a note of the best episodes and descriptions.

Extension:
(a) You could use this page to make a large class picture book. Ask those who produced the best episodes and descriptions to write them up. Give these pieces of writing to others to illustrate. Mount them in the right sequence in a large book, filling in between the work with the inter-linking words from the pupil's page.
(b) Use the story outline on the pupil's page in drama.
(c) If this activity proves promising, have a go at constructing your own storyline, interspersed with talk activities, to repeat the activity.

23 What are the robots saying?

Talk expected: descriptive; imaginative; narrative.

Objectives:
(a) to stimulate imaginative thinking
(b) to stimulate descriptive language
(c) to increase interest in science-fiction.

Preparation: Talk about science-fiction stories the pupils may have seen on television or read in books. What distinguishes a science-fiction story from other stories?

Organisation:
(a) The pupils should be in threes, fours or fives.
(b) They will need pencil and paper.
(c) Read aloud the pupil's page, making sure that they are following it.
(d) Stress that the answers each group gives to the list of questions will be speculative. They are the kinds of questions that writers of science-fiction stories and playscripts will be asking themselves, and the answers will therefore have to be as interesting as can be managed. Ask groups to note down what they decide for each question.
(e) Have a reporting back session in which answers to each question are compared.
(f) Some groups may want to record their answers on tape.

Extension:
(a) A large chart could be made to display the results of this activity. The questions from the pupil's page are displayed and alongside each one is an envelope containing all the written answers thought up by each group. Pictures could illustrate the chart.
(b) Some pupils may wish to use this activity as a starting point for writing science-fiction stories.
(c) Encourage some pupils to make a display of science-fiction books, pictures and toys.

24 Just imagine – fireworks

Talk expected: descriptive; predictive; imaginative; personal.

Objective: to stimulate these types of language, using a familiar theme.

Preparation: Talk about the photograph and then consider with the pupils what Bonfire Night might be like for those who cannot see. Ask some pupils to describe a firework as if speaking to someone who has lost his/her sight.

Organisation:
(a) The pupils should be in pairs.
(b) Explain the activity. One pupil describes what he/she sees in the picture as if he/she were at the scene, the other closes his eyes and listens. Then they imagine what might happen next – for example, what other displays of fireworks they might see.
(c) Let the pairs go on to numbers 2 and 3 on their page when they are ready.
(d) Have a reporting back session on numbers 2 and 3 if this seems appropriate.

Extension: The pupils could describe and make pictures of their invented fireworks. Use this as a model for similar work. One pupil describes a picture to another who pretends blindness.

25 Robot helpers

Talk expected: descriptive; comparative; persuasive.

Objectives:
(a) to argue persuasively for and against a list of alternatives
(b) to describe and compare functions.

Preparation: Ask the pupils what they understand by the term 'robot'. How much of their response is fictional and how much is fact? Try to disentangle the two. Then ask them how they think a walking, talking robot might be invented, i.e. what is the process by which it will come into being? This will help clarify the nature of human inventions, and will lead into the activity in which the pupils role-play as inventors.

Organisation:
(a) Divide the class into threes or fours.
(b) Read aloud the pupil's page. Encourage pupils to list more than twelve household chores, so that in drawing up a final list they have to compare the merits of each item, arguing for and against them.
(c) Have a reporting back session, listing all the separate items suggested by the pupils, and then as a whole group decide (perhaps by voting) what the House-Robot should be programmed to do.
(d) Do the same with the School-Robot.
(e) The pupils could go on to draw a diagram of the robot, clearly labelled.

26 What am I thinking of?

Talk expected: descriptive; imaginative; narrative.

Objectives:
(a) to develop descriptive language
(b) to develop attentive listening
(c) to develop thinking in images.

Preparation: Point out to the pupils that you can describe things from different angles – the sides, below, above, behind and in front – and each description could be quite different. Furthermore, descriptions are often given in terms of what the image reminds one of, using metaphor and simile. An example of this is given on the pupil's page, where an elephant is described in terms of metaphors. These two ideas form the basis of the game.

Organisation:
(a) The pupils should be in pairs.
(b) Ask the pairs to spend a couple of minutes matching the two columns on their page.
(c) As a whole group, discuss which angle matches which description, and talk about the appropriateness of each. Point out that each description shows what the author is *reminded of* when he looks at these angles of an elephant.
(d) Choose another object which has interesting possibilities and do the same thing, writing the descriptions on the board. Have the pupils got the idea?
(e) Explain the game.
(f) Circulate while it is being played, checking that the descriptions given use simile and metaphor. Some pupils may have initial difficulty in thinking of an object, so carry a list with you to give them a suggestion. You might include on your list: horse, lorry, kettle, bottle, shoe, tablelamp, goldfish, pencil-sharpener, desk, etc.

Extension:
(a) This is a good idea for writing poetry – a verse for each angle – which can be presented as riddles.
(b) It can also be a theme in art, where an object is drawn from the various angles and presented as one picture.

27 Form your own club

Talk expected: various.

Objective: to encourage pupils to form discussion groups which meet regularly to share a common interest.

Preparation: Explain to the pupils that people of all ages enjoy forming clubs to share common interests. Some of their parents and relatives might belong to such groupings – which would include evening classes, book clubs, etc. What clubs do any of the pupils belong to, e.g. Cubs and Brownies, sports clubs, book clubs, etc.?

Organisation: You will want to launch this idea to the whole group, using the words on the pupil's page as a starting point, but you will be aware that only some pupils will actually want to, or find that they can, respond. So it is probably better to discuss the idea towards the end of a lesson period and just prior to a breaktime during which those pupils who are interested could get together to discuss it.

Therefore, read the pupil's page with all the pupils, talk about it, then tell the pupils that over the next week you hope groups of them will come to you with ideas for a club and a list of prospective members.

When this has happened, give them some lesson time to work out the details and rules of the club. Keep a record of the club, who is in it, when they meet, what they need, what they achieve. Inject new ideas into the club if you find that interest is waning.

You will probably find that some groups fold fairly quickly from a lack of leadership or commitment, while others sustain an interest over a lengthy period of time. Your interest and the time you are prepared to give, could be a deciding factor in the success of the clubs.

28 What if . .?

See the notes in Book 1, Unit 5 for the same type of activity.

29 The story card game

Talk expected: narrative.

Objectives:
(a) to provide a stimulus for the invention of a group story
(b) to develop storytelling
(c) to develop sequential memory.

Preparation: Make sure you have six pieces of card the size of playing cards for each pupil who is to do the activity.

Organisation:
(a) Divide the class or group into threes or fours.
(b) Read the pupil's page aloud. With the help of the pupils, see if you can continue the story on the pupil's page – in order to demonstrate the method.
(c) Give out six cards to each player. Ask the groups to decide what should be drawn on each of the cards, making a list of five objects for each pupil, so that no duplication occurs. They should then draw the objects on five of the cards, with the name of each object beside the drawing. The sixth card should be a picture of a person.
(d) The group are then ready to begin. Some of them may wish to tape their story if this proves practical. When they have reached the end of their story – which need not mean that all the cards are used up – they should repeat it together and then tell it to you.
(e) If this activity proves successful, it can be repeated immediately or at a later date.

Extension:

(a) It may be appropriate for some of the stories to be written, or a compilation of them could be made on tape.

(b) Clearly, the pictures used could also prove useful for stimulating written stories and for improvised drama.

(c) Pictures from magazines, etc. could also be used in a similar way.

30 What's it like?

Talk expected: explanatory; descriptive; imaginative.

Objectives:

(a) to stimulate imaginative explanations involving metaphor and simile

(b) to stimulate inventive descriptions.

Preparation: Talk about the use of metaphor and simile in everyday language. Make sure you have eighteen strips of card or paper for each pair working on this.

Organisation:

(a) The pupils should be in pairs.

(b) Explain what has to be done. Give an example for the first one, e.g. 'My friend's hair is like . . . a plate of cold spaghetti.'

(c) While the pupils are matching the half-sentences, make sure they can justify to you and their partner why the match is appropriate.

(d) Listen to some of the sentences for the second part of the activity. Point out how they can be lengthened with the addition of adjectives, adverbs and subordinate clauses.

Extension:

(a) Can the pupils write their own metaphors and similes instead of the ones given? If so, pairs could share their results with other pairs.

(b) Which pair can write and say the longest sentence to complete any of the stems given on the second half of the pupil's page?

31 What will happen next?

Talk expected: narrative.

Objectives: story invention and storytelling in groups.

Organisation:

(a) Divide the class into threes or fours.

(b) Read the story aloud. Make sure the pupils can follow it as you read.

(c) Talk briefly about the possibilities of each 'instant' quality.

(d) Ask the groups to have a go, using Myra and her INSTANT CLEVERNESS.

(e) Have some reporting back on this. Suggest how it can be improved. Will it help the pupils to make notes, such as a plot-line, for their story?

(f) If the idea promises to be successful with most of the pupils, ask them to

continue the story using one or more of the other three characters.
(g) Report back if appropriate. Some could record their work on tape.

Extension:
(a) Some pupils may want to write their stories down.
(b) Some of their stories could be used in improvised drama.
(c) You could read them the last story in Margaret Mahy's popular collection of short stories for children: *The Chewing-Gum Rescue and Other Stories*, (Methuen Magnet paperback); it uses the idea of instant powders and the effect they have on people in a town.

32 Think of a chimpanzee!

Talk expected: descriptive; comparative; narrative.

Objectives:
(a) to explore through language what it means to be human
(b) to make comparisons
(c) to stimulate storytelling.

Preparation: Talk about the photograph on the pupil's page, pointing out that chimpanzees are nearest to us on the evolutionary scale. If you can display other pictures of chimpanzees this will help to stimulate interest. Ask the pupils if they have seen these animals in zoos and ask them to describe what they saw.

Organisation:
(a) The pupils should work in pairs.
(b) They will need to record the similarities and differences on paper in two columns. Explain this, giving an example of each column.
(c) When the discussion is coming to an end, compile with the class on the board or on large sheets of paper a list of all the similarities and differences the pupils have found.
(d) Encourage them to make up a story in which they have a chimpanzee as a pet for the day.
(e) Pairs may want to report back on their stories; one or two might want to tape theirs.

Extension:
(a) Some pairs may wish to write their chimpanzee stories.
(b) The stories could be used as a basis for improvised drama.
(c) If you found this activity successful, repeat, using other pictures.

33 Aesop's Fables

Talk expected: interpretative; persuasive.

Objectives:
(a) to interest pupils in the fable form

(b) to give opportunities for interpretative discussion

(c) to argue persuasively for one's point of view.

Preparation: You could read some fables to the class or group in the days before this activity, and discuss the nature of its form and its use of a summative moral. It is not necessary to do this but it will mean that the pupils will approach this activity with more understanding and confidence. (See Book 1, Unit 30, and Book 2, Unit 31, for more Aesop's fables.)

Organisation:

(a) The pupils should be in groups of three or four.

(b) Read aloud the first fable. Make sure the pupils can follow it and can refer back to it. Explain that of the morals given any might fit. Ask the group to discuss each one and come to some agreement if possible on which they think best expresses the meaning of the fable. The answer is deliberately ambiguous to stimulate argument, and there is therefore likely to be disagreement when the pupils report back. Always insist that the pupils give reasons for their answers. During the reporting back a consensus should emerge on which of the morals is strongest – and so I resist the temptation to say which I think is the best of the five.

(c) Do the same for the second fable.

(d) The last two fables have no moral and it is the task of the group to think of a suitable one for each. When they report back, write the best of their morals on the board and then ask the groups to reconsider their ideas with these alternatives in mind. Does a consensus emerge after this on what are the best morals for these two fables?

Extension:

(a) This activity can be repeated by reading aloud other fables and asking the pupils to think of a moral to go with each.

(b) Fables make good subjects for art work, especially when presented in the form of a picture sequence.

(c) Can some pupils have a go at writing fables?

(d) Because of the brevity of the fable form, fables are useful for retelling by the pupils in their own words. Ask the pupils to get to know a fable well and then retell it to a group or to the whole class.

(e) Because of the strong moral flavour of most fables, they can make a useful contribution to assemblies in the form of readings, acting and retellings.

34 Can you describe a person?

Talk expected: descriptive.

Objectives:

(a) to develop the ability to give accurate descriptions

(b) to test and develop memory.

Preparation: Collect together pictures of people, using old magazines and photographs, etc. Mount these on card. Alternatively, as suggested in the pupil's book, ask the children to find for themselves pictures of people in books and magazines. Photographs are preferable to drawings for this.

Organisation:
(a) The pupils should be in groups of four to six.
(b) Make sure each group has enough pictures for each activity i.e. at least three pictures per pupil.
(c) Read the instructions on the pupil's page for the first activity.
(d) Ask each pupil to take a picture and examine it in silence for one minute, which you time. The picture is then turned over.
(e) Each pupil has to try and describe the picture without looking at it again. The rest of the group have the picture in front of them. When the description is over, the pupil should be allowed to see the picture again to find out how accurate the description was.
(f) If there are enough pictures, let the pupils each have a second go at this.
(g) Have a reporting back session to see how the pupils now assess their ability to describe from memory.
(h) Next, they try the second activity on the pupil's page. One of the group must be the police officer who asks for the descriptions. Again, time the pupils for two minutes while they look in silence at the set of pictures in front of them.
(i) Report back on this. How are the pupils doing?
(j) Move on to the third activity – perhaps reserving a set of pictures for it so that the pupils come to them entirely fresh. Time them for twenty seconds after the pictures have been turned over in the group.
(k) Finally, ask each group to think about what they have learned from this about the efficiency of their memory. What implications does this work have for police enquiries?

35 Sarah and the storyteller

Talk expected: narrative; interpretative.

Objectives:
(a) to develop storytelling
(b) to reconstruct a folktale based on notes.

Preparation:
(a) You could read the pupils a folktale and then present its main events in the form of a plot-line on the board to illustrate what Sarah has done on the pupil's page.
(b) Have ready a number of collections of short folk and fairy tales and fables for the second activity.

Organisation:
(a) The pupils should be in pairs or threes.
(b) Read the pupil's page with them down to the end of the first task. Start the story off with them if you wish, to show that the few words in Sarah's notes have to be brought alive and greatly expanded, with plenty of vivid detail.
(c) Circulate, listening in to the reconstructions, giving help where necessary.
(d) If some groups finish before others, listen to their stories.
(e) Combine groups so that each hears at least one other version of the same story. Does any group want to retell its story to the whole class?

(f) The second activity is best done in pairs. The pupils make notes for the plot of a short story, then pass them on to another pair who try and reconstruct it. Both story and reconstruction could then be recorded on the same tape for others to listen to.

Extension:
(a) Use a plot-line to stimulate reconstruction of a story through acting in drama.
(b) Plot-lines can also stimulate written stories.
(c) If you want to develop story retellings, ask pupils to make a plot-line summary of a story and then use it to retell the story in their own words.

36 Who do you agree with?

Talk expected: persuasive.

Objectives:
(a) to develop and argue a point of view
(b) to consider the views of others.

Preparation:
(a) Ask the pupils what jobs they are expected to do around the home.
(b) Take a count of the pets pupils have.

Organisation:
(a) The pupils should be in groups of two to four.
(b) Read aloud the first section on the pupil's page.
(c) Let the pupils discuss this, then report back, looking at each item on Alex's list. What other jobs could he have included?
(d) Read aloud the second section on the pupil's page and ask them to discuss in groups who they agree with. Again, report back, perhaps taking a vote.

Extension: The more able pupils might be able to write short texts like the one about pets for discussion. The formula is simple: two people holding opposite views on a subject are contrasted. Their views should be expressed in one or two simple sentences, some in dialogue. These texts could then be used by the rest of the class.

Teacher's Notes for

The SPOKEN WORD Project

Book 3:
Talk it Through

(for Upper Junior pupils)

1 Golden Rules for talking in groups

This page appears in all three course books. Please refer to teacher's notes for Book 1 (p. 18).

2 To start you talking

Talk expected: comparative; imaginative; explanatory.

Objectives:
(a) to make pupils aware of the kinds of talk they use and will need in the future
(b) to help them compare the four types of verbal communication.

Preparation:
(a) Find out if the pupils have done the second activity in Books 1 and 2 which considers the four aspects of verbal communication: reading, writing, talking and listening. Recap on this if they have; if not, consider using one or both of the activities.
(b) If the pupils have not done this kind of work before, explain to them the nature of the course.

Organisation:
(a) The class or group should be divided into pairs or small discussion groups.
(b) Read with them the pupil's page as far as the end of number 1. Talk about the uses of reading, writing, talking and listening, then ask groups to discuss which they think they will need most in their lives. (Refer to the teacher's notes for Unit 2 in Books 1 and 2.)
(c) With the pupils, read number 2 on the pupil's page. If you wish, elaborate on the definitions given – but do not pre-empt the pupils' group discussion by doing so.
(d) Have a trial run with the first three definitions ('Explain' has been done for you), then report back to make sure that the pupils know what to do. Make sure that examples from more than one group are given for each type of talk.
(e) Do the same for the next three – or let the pupils discuss all the rest and have a fairly lengthy reporting back session at the end.
(f) To sum up, take a vote on number 3 on the pupil's page.

Extension: You may feel that the pupils would benefit from a revision of this work a few days later. You could read or say something (e.g a little story or a recipe) and ask the pupils to classify it using the twelve types of speech explored here.

3 What a riddle!

Talk expected: interpretative.

Objectives:
(a) to stimulate interpretative discussion in which reference to detail is important
(b) to stimulate interest in the riddle form.

Preparation: The pupils may well have attempted to solve the riddles in Books 1 and 2 of this course, and by this age they should be reasonably familiar with the form. If not, find some fairly easy riddles to try out with them so that they come to this page prepared.

Organisation:
(a) The pupils should work in pairs.
(b) Stress that every clue in the riddle has to fit the solution offered. The first riddle is relatively easy, to give quick success; the rest are less easy and may well baffle some if not most of the pupils, but in the process of trying to solve them much discussion could be generated. Make sure that the pupils do not call out their solutions until the reporting back session. The solutions the author had in mind are as follows, but alternatives are welcomed if all the clues fit.
Riddle 1: the sound of a church bell
Riddle 2: water
Riddle 3: a book
Riddle 4: car tyres
(c) When pairs report back make sure they give a full justification for their answers; don't forget to invite alternative suggestions.

Extension
(a) The pupils should have a go at writing their own riddles for others to try to solve.
(b) Find some riddles and write them on card for a pinboard display or riddle box, both of which could stimulate interpretative discussion.

4 Are ghosts real?

Talk expected: interpretative; persuasive.

Objectives:
(a) to stimulate a discussion about a controversial subject
(b) to interpret two poems.

Preparation: The subject of ghosts is a particularly useful one for discussion with pupils, since not only is it a subject in which most are interested, it is also a controversial area, half-way between fact and fantasy. It is a subject which encourages children to confront the nature of evidence and what can count as fact, but goes beyond that into the area of non-rational belief; and it allows for opposing views.

To begin, ask the pupils if they have any first-hand or second-hand experience of ghosts. This will lead on to the questions: How do we know about ghosts? Is it all fantasy? What are they? Could they exist? etc.

Organisation:
(a) Decide if you want the whole class to work simultaneously on this or whether you want small group work throughout. The former allows you to hold a full class debate on the main motion suggested at the end of the pupil's page.
(b) Talk about the photograph. Are photographs purporting to be of ghosts sufficient evidence of the existence of ghosts? If not, what are the motives

behind the production of trick photographs? The latter question could be discussed in small groups and then shared with the rest of the class.

(c) Read the first poem, 'A Ghostly Bed', which is rather tongue-in-cheek. It might help the pupils to visualise the scene of the poem if you drew a sketch on the board showing an empty grave and a headstone with a name on it. Having read the poem, ask groups to discuss the following question: Did a ghost come out of the grave?

(d) Read the poem 'The Coward' to the class. Beforehand, sketch in the historical background, i.e. a ruined cottage is said to be haunted by the ghost of Susan Lewin who was murdered – so the story goes – by Roundheads (Cromwell's soldiers) because she was part of a Royalist household which had harboured an important Royalist. The writer of the poem goes to investigate the haunting, 'talks' to the ghost of Sue, but when he 'sees' the ghosts of the two Roundheads he flees.

Once you have read the poem to the class, write the following questions on the board and ask groups of 3–5 to discuss them, reporting back at the end:
(1) What happened when the poet reached the ruined cottage?
(2) What did he mean when he said at the end, 'Forgive me, my Sue"?
(3) Could this happen in real life – to you, perhaps?

(e) By now the pupils should be ready to hold a class debate – or more small group discussions – on the motion: 'Ghosts are real'. Speakers for and against should be appointed if a class debate is opted for, and while they are preparing their speech, the rest of the class could be jotting down their own ideas. Have a vote (secret ballot?) at the end.

Extension
(a) Some of the pupils could do a survey of other children in the school, asking whether they believe in ghosts. All the pupils in the class could also gather the views of their families.
(b) Make a display of books, stories, poems, etc. about ghosts.
(c) The pupils could write poems, perhaps responding to the title *What is a Ghost?* or completing the stem: 'A ghost is . . .' for every line.

5 *What's your point of view?*

Talk expected: comparative; persuasive; interpretative.

Objectives:
(a) to interpret and compare several points of view
(b) to argue for and against points of view
(c) to encourage a more discerning approach to television programmes.

Preparation: Referring to *Radio Times* and *TV Times*, do a quick survey of what the pupils are watching on television. Talk about the BBC television programme 'Points of View' in which letters from viewers are read out. Have any of the pupils thought of writing to the programme praising or criticising something they have watched?

Organisation:
(a) Divide the class or group into pairs or small groups.
(b) With the pupils, read the opening paragraphs of the pupil's page. If the

children are familiar with a programme called 'Grange Hill', which is about life in a comprehensive school, they will understand better what the letter writers are responding to; if not, sketch in the type of programme it might be, showing life in a comprehensive school, warts and all.

(c) Ask five pupils in turn to read one of the letters aloud, repeating the letters yourself.

(d) Groups should then: (1) decide what they think the writer is saying, and (2) find reasons for and against the writer's point of view.

(e) Have a reporting back session, getting several views on each letter. You could record agreement and disagreement on the board, using ticks and crosses.

(f) By this time the pupils may well wish to have a go at writing a letter to a television company themselves, so to encourage this let them draft a letter. You can comment on it before they make a final version. They could be sent to 'Points of View' (if the programme is still being broadcast), or to the producer of the programmes concerned. Replies may be forthcoming and they would stimulate further discussion.

(g) Finally, perhaps a few days later, hold a class debate on the proposition on the pupil's page. Arrange for speakers for and against to open the debate and to sum it up. Take votes after the discussion.

6 Good wishes

Talk expected: comparative; personal; persuasive.

Objectives:
(a) to compare and evaluate moral statements
(b) to develop moral ideas and their expression.

Organisation:
(a) The pupils should discuss this in groups of two to four.
(b) Encourage them to evaluate each statement (i.e. No. 1 on their page).
(c) Have a reporting back session. Discuss the merits of each statement first and then ask pupils to go on to No. 2 and put the statements in order of importance.
(d) Record the results on the board to find out what the whole class view is.
(e) The pupils should then do No. 3 on their page. These should be shared and if possible written up and displayed.

Extension: The pupils could have a go at writing an account or a story based on one of the wishes on the pupil's page or one they have thought up themselves. For example, their opening paragraph could feature a wizard who makes the wish come true and the rest of the account tells of the consequences.

7 Can you continue the story?

Talk expected: narrative.

Objective: to develop storytelling in threes.

Preparation: Talk briefly about the different kinds of stories available: myth and legend, folk and fairy tale, fables, historical, fantasy and supernatural, contemporary realism, science-fiction, etc. A story beginning, such as the one presented on the pupil's page, could go in several of these directions and the author has to decide the kind of story to be written.

Organisation:
(a) Divide the class into threes.
(b) Read the pupil's page aloud while the children follow it. Elaborate on what could be meant by a magic story, a horror story and a science-fiction story so that the pupils are clear about the differences.
(c) Encourage the pupils to work out what happens during the three-day time-scale of their story, keeping notes of the main events. When they are clear about this, each member of the group should tell the story of one of the days. If possible, have some groups tape their stories; others can tell the class theirs if they are confident enough.

Extension:
(a) The stories could be written by the groups and made into individual books.
(b) Read parts of Helen Cresswell's *A Gift From Winklesea* (Puffin) and Penelope Lively's *Dragon Trouble* (Banana Books, Heinemann), both of which use the idea of a mysterious egg hatching into something unusual.

8 Can you complete these similes?

Talk expected: comparative; interpretative; explanatory.

Objective: to explore the use of simile.

Preparation:
(a) Make sure you have 32 slips of paper for each pair of pupils.
(b) Introduce the idea of simile, i.e. we compare one thing with another to heighten its meaning. Ask the pupils to complete in as many ways as they can the stem: 'I was as cold as . . .' and 'I was as hot as . . .'. This will illustrate what simile does and how prevalent it is in daily speech.

Organisation:
(a) The pupils should work in pairs.
(b) Explain what is required. It is better if each pupil in the pair writes out eight items from each list; encourage them to talk about the stems and similes as they copy them.
(c) Some of the similes make a clear match with the stems, but others are purposely ambiguous, to stimulate discussion. The items can be moved around in order to arrive at the best final arrangement. While the pupils are doing the matching, circulate and ask them to justify some of their matchings.
   The ones the author had in mind follow, but variations are, of course, permissible.

   I was as snug as a bird in an egg beneath its mother.

   I was as silent as a room without a doorway.

I was as dazed as a hungry pigeon half-frozen in the snow.

I was as happy as a child whose last worry had vanished.

I was as slow as a tree growing in dry soil.

I was as puzzled as a Martian at a fairground.

I was as faint as a cool and fading moonbeam.

I was as tough as the heart of a stone in a dark mine.

I was as intelligent as the minds of ten old wizards.

I was as angry as a dragon in a cage.

I was as sad as a man who had lost his last hope.

I was as tired as a sleigh-dog trekking across the Arctic snow.

I was as old as my first breath.

I was as pale as a mushroom in a cellar.

I was as wise as the world's best poems.

I was as quick as the change of a snowflake in a flame.

(d) Next, pairs have to argue which sentences they feel are exaggerated. Again, report back on this.
(e) The game suggested at the end of the pupil's page encourages pupils to search for and use similes in their own speech.

Extension:
(a) Draw attention to the use of simile in the poems and stories you are reading to the pupils.
(b) Have a simile chart on the wall on which pupils write similes as they come across them in talk and in reading.
(c) Use similes as the basis for drawings and picture making.

9 What should Angela do?

Talk expected: persuasive; comparative; predictive; imaginative.

Objective: to argue for and against a set of alternative courses of action.

Preparation: Some of the pupils are likely to have elderly friends or relatives who may be in frail health. Ask them to tell the group or class about these people. Lead into the story on the pupil's page by asking: 'What would happen if you were alone with your elderly friend or relative and they were suddenly taken ill?'

Organisation:
(a) The pupils should work in groups of three to five.
(b) Read aloud the story below. Make sure that the pupils follow the picture version of it on their page.
(c) Ask one person in each group to retell the story in his or her own words to the rest of the group, using the pictures.

(d) Groups should then discuss a number of alternative courses of action which Angela could take. They should make a note of them, with reasons for and against, to help in reporting back.

(e) Have a full reporting back session, listing on the board the most sensible suggestions. Which course of action will the pupils collectively feel is the most sensible?

Extension: This story makes a clear contribution to health education, and it is an effective way of teaching practical aspects of the subject. You could use the same discussion technique by asking the pupils what Angela should do if, for example: (1) she saw a person who appeared to be drowning in a river, (2) she witnessed a serious road accident, and (3) she scalded herself with boiling water.

Angela and her grandma

Angela visited her grandma twice a week after school. Grandma lived in a farm cottage down a long winding country lane. They enjoyed each other's company very much and grandma came to rely on Angela's visits for companionship and help.

Grandma, however, was not very well. She was old, and if she did not take the various pills given to her by her doctor she would soon become ill. Angela knew this, but they did not talk about it.

They would talk about their family and school and Angela would read to her grandma. After that they had a delicious tea.

On this particular Tuesday, Angela put the key in the lock as usual, opened the door and called out to her grandma. She would usually answer from the living-room where she would be listening to the radio or reading. But on this day Angela heard a strange, faint cry: 'Help me, Ange.' It came from upstairs.

Alarmed, Angela rushed upstairs and found her grandma lying on the bathroom floor. She had slipped and fallen that morning, and there was so much pain she feared she had broken her hip. She could only whisper very faintly.

'Get me my pills,' she implored.

Angela dashed into the bedroom. There were about six bottles of different pills on the bedside cabinet. 'Which ones?' she called out. There was no answer. Grandma had fainted.

What was Angela to do?

There was no telephone in the house and she couldn't remember where the nearest telephone box was. Her own house was a good twenty-minute run away, and besides, there would be no one there. She did not know any of the neighbours – in fact, there were hardly any – and she was a little frightened of knocking on a stranger's door in this lonely place.

She stood in the bedroom, near panic, unable to decide what to do. Time was running out for grandma. She had to do something fast.

What do you think Angela should do?

10 Can you solve the mystery?

Talk expected: interpretative; persuasive; imaginative.

Objectives:
(a) to construct through discussion a solution to a mystery
(b) to develop an interest in poetry.

Preparation: Explain to the pupils that this poem contains a mystery – as indicated in the title – but no solution is supplied by the poet. The reader has to be the detective and construct one or more plausible scenarios to explain what might have happened. Besides this, we do not know who Lulu is, who is telling the story, and whether or not we are dealing with a broken family.

Organisation:
(a) The pupils should work in groups of two to four.
(b) Read the poem to them while they follow it in their books. Then ask them to look at each verse in turn and work out what they think is happening. Finally, they should attempt to solve the problem of Lulu's disappearance.
(c) Have a reporting back session. Several possible solutions should be forthcoming – record these on the board. Do not accept anything which is contradicted by the poem.

Extension: Some pupils may wish to use this work as the context for a piece of writing. For example, they could write an account of Lulu's experiences that night; or what happens to the character who is telling the story in the poem when he/she sets out to find Lulu.

11 News Review

Talk expected: various, with the emphasis upon reporting and performance skills.

Objectives:
(a) to gain experience in working in a small planning and production team
(b) to consider the press in relation to a particular audience
(c) to edit, summarise, and deliver short texts
(d) to gain experience of interviewing
(e) to gain an insight into radio news programmes.

Preparation: Three things are essential for this idea:
(1) newspapers, local and national – but not all will be suitable reading for children of this age so it is better to vet them yourself before passing them on to the pupils; nevertheless, a request to the class for newspapers could bring in all you need;
(2) a quiet space for the pupils to record interviews and the final tape;
(3) time for pupils to do the activity satisfactorily – many skills are involved in this, and much could be learned, but it cannot be done without generous provision of time, which may well cut across any fixed timetable you work to.

Organisation:
(a) You could have groups of four to six pupils working on this, one group per week to cover the preceding week's news.
(b) Talk to this group in detail about the 'News Review', using the pupil's page as a guide. Work out a stage by stage plan, record it on a flow-chart, and ask the pupils to report to you on completion of each stage so that you can keep track of progress.
(c) Select an item of interest from a newspaper and show the group how to turn it into a short, direct text for the tape. Point out that such stories can be enlivened by (mock) interviews with the people in the news report. Obviously, the readability level of the newspaper report should be within the pupils' grasp.
(d) If you have time, listen to a rehearsal of the final script and suggest improvements where necessary.
(e) Make sure the rest of the class hear the tape. The group who made it can report on their experience of putting it together after the broadcast.

12 Can you give a talk?

Talk expected: various, with the emphasis upon reporting and/or persuasive talk, and on performance skills.

Objective: to give pupils the experience of preparing a talk of their own choice and delivering it to an audience of peers.

Organisation:
(a) Decide whether you want *all* the pupils in the class to have a go at this. Bear in mind that for some particularly shy pupils this may be too daunting and cause undue anxiety. (One way of overcoming this problem, of course, is to tape the pupil's talk to play to the class later.) Decide, also, whether you will allow pupils to work in pairs or more for this if they request it.
(b) Draw up a list of the pupils' names big enough for display, like this:

NAME	SUBJECT OF TALK	DATE GIVEN

When the pupils are ready, fill in the list. Give the pupils as much time as they need, spreading the talks over a term or more.
(c) Stress that talks can be on various subjects: hobbies, outings, enthusiasms, making things, books read, ideas and arguments, etc.
(d) Go through the pupil's talk beforehand to see that everything is accurate and well-prepared.
(e) Tape the talk if this is feasible and if it does not make the pupil feel even more self-conscious. It can be listened to again by all those who might be interested in the subject or the child.

13 What if . .?

See the notes for Book 1, Unit 5 (p. 21) for the same type of activity.

14 Who do you agree with?

Talk expected: persuasive.

Objectives:
(a) to evaluate opposing points of view
(b) to discuss sexist and non-sexist attitudes
(c) to give one's own point of view and develop it in discussion.

Preparation: This discussion activity considers sexist assumptions that help shape children's lives and attitudes. Granny represents an attitude which is gradually disappearing but is still in evidence, and the pupils will be familiar with some of the things she is saying.
   You can help prepare the pupils for the issues they are going to discuss by: (1) finding out whether they have done *The Wrestling Princess* activity in Book 2 of the course, and if they have not, consider using it; (2) asking their views on whether they think there are actions which are specifically for boys/men and girls/women and why they hold these views, and (3) reading them non-sexist stories of which there are a growing number on the market. For example, see:
Browne, Anthony: *Piggybook*, Anderson 1986, a picture book for all ages
Impey, Rose: *Who's a Clever Girl, Then*? Heinemann Banana Books 1986
Kemp, Gene: *The Turbulent Term of Tyke Tiler*, Puffin 1979
Paola, Tomi de: *Oliver Button is a Sissy*, Methuen 1981
Williams, Jay: *The Practical Princess and Other Stories*, Hippo Books 1983.

Organisation:
(a) The pupils should be in groups of three to five.
(b) Appoint someone to play the part of Diane and another to play David. You can play Granny.
(c) Read aloud the first one and discuss Gran's statement.
(d) Groups should do the same, discussing whether they agree or disagree with Diane and Gran.
(e) Ask the groups to discuss the rest of Gran's conversations with Diane, then report back if appropriate.
(f) Do the same with Gran's conversations with David.
(g) As suggested at the end of the pupil's page, the pupils could each write a short conversation between Gran and the twins and then discuss this in their groups.

Extension:
(a) Write on large strips of paper some statements, both sexist amd non-sexist, which have emerged from the above work, arrange these in random order on a pinboard with the title: 'Which do you agree with?' This will help to keep the discussion alive over a longer period.
(b) Some pupils could interview members of their family about their perceptions of male and female roles, preparing their questions beforehand and presenting their results to the class if this is appropriate.

15 Can you tell a story?

Talk expected: narrative.

Objective: to give pairs the stimulus to invent and tell a story to another pair.

Preparation: Explain that essential ingredients for a story are: characters, setting and events; that once these have been created you have the bones of a story. The lists on the pupil's page suggest examples of these ingredients, with the addition of a list of objects or 'story props'. Combinations of items from the lists will give the pupils the bones of a story – the skill is in the weaving of a narrative around them.

Organisation:
(a) The pupils should work in pairs.
(b) Explain the method, and if possible give a short impromptu example of how it works in practice, i.e. tell a short story.
(c) It would be better for the pairs if they wrote on slips of paper those items from each list they have chosen to use, and then, putting the book aside, lay these in front of them, providing the basis for their story. Emphasise the need for descriptive detail.
(d) When they feel they have a story good enough for another pair to listen to, they should put their hands up and at your signal join another prepared pair to share their story with. There can, of course, be many combinations of pairs.
(e) Is there any pair who would like to tell their story to the whole class?
(f) If there is time, more than one attempt at a story can be made, and this page can, of course, be used more than once.

Extension: Some of the stories could well be acted or written, and the lists on the pupil's page could be used for these activities too.

16 The 'Why?' game

Talk expected: questioning; explanatory.

Objectives:
(a) to give pupils experience in sustained questioning and interviewing
(b) to encourage pupils to follow a line of argument to its logical conclusion
(c) to help pupils 'think aloud'.

Organisation:
(a) The pupils should work in pairs.
(b) Read aloud the instructions on the pupil's page.
(c) If you are confident enough, give a demonstration of this, answering a succession of 'whys?' from a pupil to show what is meant.
(d) Let the pupils have a trial run and report back on how it went.

Extension: Some pupils might like the idea of writing down the question and answer sequence to see how long they can make it, perhaps using computer paper if this is available.

17 What's your opinion?

Talk expected: personal; comparative; persuasive; explanatory; descriptive; imaginative.

Objective: to consider abstract sculpture in small discussion groups and develop the above types of talk.

Preparation: It would help if you assembled a collection of pictures – slides and postcards are particularly useful – of abstract art, so that the pupils are discussing the sculptures presented on their page in this wider context. Talk about the modern artist's concern with shape, colour, texture, space and form, expressed in an abstract, non-realistic way.

Organisation:
(a) The pupils can work in pairs or threes.
(b) They should discuss each question in turn, jotting down a summary of their responses if you like.
(c) Have a reporting back session and go through each question, listening to a variety of responses.

Extension: Explore the theme of abstract art and modelling further, encouraging the pupils to have a go at making abstract art themselves – if, of course, they feel reasonably positive about it, which may not be the case!

18 Sarah's dream

Talk expected: comparative; persuasive; imaginative.

Objectives:
(a) to make comparisons between fantasy and reality
(b) to argue for and against the ideas in the 'dream'
(c) to imagine other ideas and possibilities.

Preparation: Talk about how common it is for us all to dream sometimes of a better world in which our ideals are more fully realised.

Organisation:
(a) Divide the class into pairs or small groups.
(b) Read out Sarah Hughes' dream on the pupil's page. It is a genuine piece and can be found in *Dear World*, an invaluable and fascinating collection of writing and art by children from around the world, edited by Richard and Helen Exley, published by Exley Publications.
(c) Explain the four questions at the end.
(d) As the pupils discuss these questions, circulate and give help where necessary. The pupils will almost certainly wish to record the differences they find and give a tick or cross to signify their attitude towards them. They may also wish to list other differences for question 4.
(e) Report back, making a list on the board from the pupils' contributions and recording the agreement and disagreement levels with ticks and crosses. Then

list other differences which come from question 4.

(f) Groups could then discuss this latter list in a similar way.

Extension:
(a) Some pupils could write their 'dreams' of a better world, others could draw a series of pictures depicting items in their visions of a better world.
(b) This is a good subject for poetry writing.
(c) The theme of a better world is a fruitful one for a class assembly.

19 Three Boys and the Head

Talk expected: persuasive; descriptive; plus performance skills in reading aloud.

Objectives:
(a) to give experience of group reading of a playscript
(b) to encourage pupils to evaluate the attitudes and motives of characters in a script
(c) to encourage pupils to imagine and describe characters.

Preparation: The pupils will take to this activity more readily if they have had experience of working from a playscript, of which there are many on the market now for group reading in the primary school; but this is not essential.

Organisation:
(a) The pupils should work in groups of four.
(b) Read the opening paragraph aloud and then ask groups to sort out who is going to play the parts of Head, John, Peter and Matthew.
(c) You may wish to participate in the initial reading, with the rest of the class listening – if so, have three fluent readers take on the parts of the children and you take on the Head's part, and read it aloud this way; then encourage groups to re-read it themselves so that the two readings will give a good working familiarity with the script.
(d) Explain what is required from the questions at the end of the script.
(e) Some pupils may have difficulty with number 2 and may need you to prompt them.
(f) Have a reporting back session.

Extension: Encourage pupils to write short scripts like this in which a figure of authority (e.g. police officer, parent, traffic warden, doctor, teacher, vicar, etc.) is lecturing one or two other characters who have done wrong. The question the pupils should end their script with is: 'How sensible were the ideas of . . . in this play?' – which can be discussed by other pupils who perform or read it.

20 Inventions

Talk expected: persuasive; comparative; imaginative; explanatory; predictive.

Objectives:
(a) to encourage pupils to examine the implications of a number of 'inventions'

(b) to compare the pros and cons of each
(c) to make predictions about the future needs of society.

Organisation:
(a) The pupils should work in pairs or threes.
(b) Read the opening paragraph on the pupil's page and talk briefly about each 'invention' so that the pupils are clear about the task.
(c) Demonstrate on the board what is meant by PRO and CONTRA lists; ask pupils to make these lists for each 'invention'.
(d) Have a trial run with 'Flying bicycles'.
(e) Report back when all six have been discussed and record final lists of three from each group on the board. Does a favourite emerge?
(f) The groups could then go on to think of other inventions that could land on the director's desk. They should describe them in detail, say what the implications of them might be and what the pros and cons are.

Extension: The pupils could record some of their ideas from (f) in drawing and writing, perhaps making a class book or display board called 'Our Inventions for the Future'. A few might want to make models of their inventions.

21 How did they find this treasure?

Talk expected: narrative; questioning.

Objectives:
(a) to develop storytelling
(b) to develop the skills of interviewing.

Organisation:
(a) Divide the class or group into fours. Three of them are to be the storytellers, the fourth to be the interviewing journalist.
(b) Discuss in general terms the sort of story the picture suggests – an adventure story, perhaps, or a ghost or time-slip story.
(c) While the storytelling trio are working out their story, the journalist must compile a list of questions to ask them.
(d) Some groups might like to report back, either by retelling their story or reanswering their interviewer's questions. Others could be given the opportunity to tape their interviews.

Extension: The stories could be written up as newspaper reports, using headlines.

22 Sort out what you say

Talk expected: persuasive; explanatory; instructive.

Objectives:
(a) to give experience of basic classification of speech
(b) to argue for or against such classification

(c) to explore the differences between fact and fantasy and what might constitute evidence

(d) to gain group experience of creating and playing a word game.

Preparation: Each group of four players will need fifty playing-card sized pieces of plain card, plus four pieces a little larger.

Organisation:

(a) Decide how many groups you want to play this at once. (Groups should be in fours.) It might be better to have a trial run with just two groups to see how the pupils take to an activity which will probably be new to them.

(b) Go through the four groups of statements explained on the pupil's page and elaborate on each category with further examples if you wish. When you have done this, ask the pupils if there is any category which still puzzles them and explain further if necessary.

(c) The groups should then have a go at classifying the list of statements on the pupil's page. Several of the statements are ambiguous in that two answers are appropriate, so explain this. The classification the author has in mind is as follows:

Statement	Group
A sheet of paper is very thin	1
A car can think.	4
All boys like porridge.	3 or 4
A bridge can span a river.	1
Cats like to hide in boxes.	2
A motorcycle is more dangerous than a car.	1 or 2
My neighbour has a flying carpet.	4
Dragons exist in Cornwall.	4
Girls are good at sums.	1 or 2
Chairs are usually comfortable.	2 or 3
Tomorrow it is sure to rain.	3
Peeling onions makes your eyes water.	2
Most ten-year-olds in Britain like school.	1 or 2
God exists.	2, 3 or 4 (but not 1 because of a lack of truth criteria)
My aunt saw a live fairy when she was a girl.	4
Girls cry more than boys.	3

(d) Report back on the groups' classifications, making sure that they can justify their answers when challenged.

(e) If they have done reasonably well so far, they are ready to play the game. Read the rules and explain them if necessary. It is better if statements are written in rough on paper first and checked by you before being written on the playing cards.

(f) Sit with each group a little while as they play the game, encouraging them to ask for help from the others in the group if they are doubtful about the classification to make. The winner must, of course, explain each of the six cards he/she has laid down.

Extension: In any spare moments make a statement to the class or to individuals and ask them to classify it as above. This will help to keep the idea fresh.

23 What would you do?

Talk expected: persuasive, comparative.

Objectives:
(a) to discuss various moral options open to a character in a story
(b) to consider the subject of unsuitable videos.

Preparation: Find out how many pupils have video-recorders at home and what controls there are (if any) on the kind of videos watched. Who chooses them? Are any prohibited? Has any pupil been frightened or disturbed by a video? Is it common for pupils to see videos in other children's houses which may not be allowed in their own house? What is wrong with so-called 'video nasties'?

Organisation:
(a) Divide the class into threes or fours.
(b) Read aloud the pupil's page, making sure it is being followed by the children.
(c) Explain the two methods of discussion outlined on the pupil's page and let the groups decide which they want to use.
(d) Have a reporting back session at a suitable moment. Record Good and Bad Angel points on the board.

Extension: Hold a class debate on the subject of 'unsuitable' programmes on television, film and videos. How much control should be exerted by parents?

24 Alien Intelligence

Talk expected: interpretative; explanatory; persuasive; comparative.

Objectives: to interpret the symbolic qualities of everyday objects and what they tell us of our way of life.

Preparation: Talk about the possibility – real or imagined – that somewhere in the universe another civilisation is gathering data about us. How could they gather such information and what would they make of it? What would happen if robots arrived to collect data – what would they take back, and how would they interpret it? This is the theme of this activity.

Organisation:
(a) Divide the class or group into pairs or threes.
(b) Read aloud the pupil's page. Ask what information a bottle of water is likely to give an alien who knows little about us – what hypotheses would an alien be likely to make about it?
(c) Groups should discuss the hypotheses the aliens might make about each item and whether they think the item of sufficient importance to make it a good choice.
(d) Report back on this, recording on the board some of the pupils' ideas about the items.
(e) Groups should then have a go at drawing up a second list of items. Some of these could be shared with the rest of the class.

Extension: A similar and better known version of this idea could be used as a development of this, i.e. a canister containing ten items is buried in the earth for people of the future to find *or* is sent into space for another civilisation to discover. What would the pupils include in this canister?

25 Sports Day

Talk expected: persuasive; descriptive; comparative.

Objectives:
(a) to give pupils the opportunity to discuss alternative ways of organising an important day in their school lives
(b) to argue for and against ideas
(c) to plan a Sports Day programme.

Preparation: This activity would, of course, be much more meaningful if the ideas generated by it did have a significant effect on how your school's sports day was organised. However, it is recognised that this may not be feasible and in this case it is probably better to have this discussion *after* a sports day when the memories and feelings of it are still fresh. If you hold the discussion just *before* a sports day without allowing the pupils' ideas any influence, then they may feel that your interest in their ideas is purely academic.

Organisation:
(a) The pupils should work in groups of three to six.
(b) Ask three fluent readers to read aloud the parts of Wayne, Fiona and Mark.
(c) Groups should then discuss question 1.
(d) Have a reporting back session. Ask for arguments for and against in turn for Wayne, Fiona and Mark, recording them in brief form on the board if this is possible.
(e) Groups should then go on to devise their own Sports Day programme, describing each race or activity. They should report back on this.
(f) Share the best of their ideas with other interested members of staff – can any of the ideas be incorporated into a future Sports Day?

26 The Black Hole Route 27

Talk expected: imaginative; predictive; explanatory; descriptive; narrative.

Objectives:
(a) to respond to a science-fiction story in a variety of spoken ways
(b) to participate actively in a story
(c) to develop an understanding of how stories work.

Preparation: Find out from the pupils the experience they have had – and their understanding of – science-fiction. It is likely that they have enjoyed it on television and in films, but less so in books, although comics might have been a source. What science-fiction can they remember having heard and read? What constitutes the science-fiction form? Have pupils written any science-fiction?

Organisation:
(a) The pupils should work in pairs or small groups.
(b) Explain that the story is incomplete and that questions are inserted during the narrative for them to discuss. As soon as these questions are reached the pupils' books should be turned over – or the succeeding text covered with a sheet of paper – to remove the temptation to read on and pre-empt the discussion.
(c) Read aloud down to the first question, making sure that the pupils are following the text. Groups should then spend a few minutes responding to the question, and some could report back before you go on. Continue in this way to the end.

Extension: The pupils could write science-fiction and explore what science-fiction is available in the school.

27 Can you rescue the princess?

Talk expected: narrative; imaginative; explanatory.

Objective: to stimulate problem-solving discussion.

Preparation: Talk about the familiar situation in fairy tales of a princess being captured and of the problems encountered in trying to rescue her. It is a situation which a teller of fairy tales has to solve in a satisfactory way to make a good story. This activity gives the pupils a chance to create their own fairy stories, or episodes of them.

Organisation:
(a) Divide the class into pairs or threes.
(b) Talk about the picture and read aloud the words underneath it. Ask groups to think of where the princess came from and how she was captured, and then have some reporting back.
(c) Groups should then go on to discuss the problem. Listen to them and look out for any groups which go for the briefest solution, such as, 'The prince got a magic wand and wished her out of the castle.' In fact, it might be best to ban magical solutions, or to allow them only for a second solution in each group.
(d) Have some groups report back. Discuss which solutions are most inventive and interesting and why.
(e) As suggested on the pupil's page, the children could then have a go at thinking of their own fairy tale problem, drawing it, explaining what is happening in it, and passing it on to others to solve.

Extension:
(a) Problems and written solutions could be displayed side by side on a pinboard or folded card, or in a class book.
(b) Use some of the ideas the pupils come up with in improvised drama. Give a group one of the problems as a starting point for acting a fairy tale.

28 Story links

Talk expected: narrative.

Objective: to develop storytelling in small groups.

Preparation: Each pupil will need six pieces of plain card the size of a playing-card.

Organisation:
(a) The pupils should work in threes or fours.
(b) Read the pupil's page with them and elaborate upon the method. Give an example of the method yourself if you feel confident enough about it to do so. Stress the need for lots of detail in the story – a few brief sentences are not really enough, although, of course, some pupils will not be able to manage more than that.
(c) Circulate and listen in on some of the stories. Set some more able groups a challenge – having told their story once, can they make it twice as long by adding lots of supporting details?
(d) The cards can be reshuffled and redealt to allow for more than one story from each member of the group. The cards can, of course, be used many times.
(e) Are there any pupils who want to retell their story to the whole class?

Extension: Some pupils may wish to write or record their stories.

29 The Divided Island

Talk expected: comparative; persuasive; explanatory; plus talk involved in problem-solving.

Objectives:
(a) to compare two kinds of rule systems
(b) to consider the fundamental needs and rights of people
(c) to solve a problem.

Preparation: This activity touches on two main aspects of society: rules and rights, and poses a problem which involves the issue of war. You can prepare for the first aspect by discussing with the pupils how rules are arrived at and enforced in the country generally and within your school.

Organisation:
(a) The pupils should work in groups of three to five.
(b) With the pupils following, read as far as the first question on the pupil's page. Emphasise the differences between the Purples' and Blues' ruling systems, then ask groups to discuss which they prefer and why. Have a reporting back session, listing arguments for and against on the board.
(c) Explain the second task. Emphasise that the civil rights they are to discuss will revolve around basic physical needs, security and freedom. The Charters should be drafted during discussion and written up later. Have a full reporting back session. Record on the board any promises you are doubtful about and ask

groups to discuss them. Allow pupils to use ideas from other groups to complete their Charters.
(d) Groups should now discuss the conflict problem. Stress that you favour a solution which sheds as little blood as possible and one which effectively reduces the chance of further conflict. Groups should share their ideas when all of them are ready.

Extension:
(a) Some pupils might like to write a story based on their ideas for solving the conflict problem.
(b) Staying with the theme of the island, how would the groups develop tourism on the island? They could devise an advertising campaign.

30 What does it mean?

Talk expected: interpretative; imaginative; personal.

Objective: to discuss meanings within a poem.

Preparation: The pupils will, of course, find this easier to discuss if they are used to hearing, reading and sharing poetry as part of the regular activities of the classroom.

Organisation:
(a) The pupils should work in pairs or threes.
(b) Explain that the poet is looking at parts of himself and is reminded of the history of his race as well as his own personal history.
(c) Read aloud the poem with the pupils listening, then again with the pupils following it in their books.
(d) To help to start the discussion, explain the first verse, i.e. when the poet looks at his hand he sees some of the things it has achieved in history; this is a metaphorical device which some pupils will not understand until it is explained to them. The same device is used in the second verse; thereafter the verses are personal.
(e) In reporting back, ask for several interpretations of each verse so that different understandings and shades of meaning can be explored.

Extension: The pupils could write their own 'My History' poems, using the first two lines of each verse of the poem discussed, and then adding their own thoughts to complete the verses.

31 Aesop's Fables

See notes for Book 1, Unit 30, (p. 39), and Book 2, Unit 33, (p. 66), both of which deal with a similar activity.

32 Can you interview someone?

Talk expected: various, but including questioning, descriptive, explanatory, personal, with an emphasis on performing skills.

Objectives:
(a) to give experience of collaborative group work involving a good deal of planning and preparation
(b) to provide opportunities for interviewing
(c) to encourage pupils to describe and explain personal enthusiasms
(d) to give experience of creating a 'radio' tape for a particular audience.

Organisation:
(a) It is probably better to have only one or two groups working on this at any one time, so select the pupils for this first.
(b) Read with the whole class the pupil's page, then introduce the one or two groups who have been chosen to create the programme. They will be looking for pupils to interview about their enthusiasms. The class could spend a few minutes discussing anything they are interested in, and then volunteers could be asked for. Record these.
(c) The rest of the class should then move on to other work while you talk to the group(s) who are going to do the programme. Base your discussion around the points made on the pupil's page. Ask them to keep you informed of the progress of the programme, particularly at the planning stage. Also, consider whether pupils from other classes might not be interviewees.
(d) When the programme is complete, listen to it beforehand to decide whether it is good enough for general broadcast in the school.
(e) If the idea works well, allow other groups to have a go.

33 Compare these beginnings

Talk expected: comparative; interpretative; persuasive; personal.

Objectives:
(a) to discuss what makes a good opening to a novel or short story
(b) to explore differing viewpoints.

Preparation:
(a) Discuss with the pupils what they think makes a good book. What sort of things are they looking for in a good read: attractive characters to identify with, villains, adventure, humour, suspense, imagination . . .? Explain that one of the best ways of sampling a book is to read the first page – does it hold the attention, promise an interesting read, make you want to turn the page? This activity will help pupils to evaluate the first page of a novel effectively and at the same time raise questions about style and genre and the skill of the writer in anticipating what the majority of readers require. You can, if you like, use real books instead of the extracts on the pupil's page, but it would be

difficult to find sufficient copies of a variety of stories to allow pupils to discuss them in groups.
(b) Look to see if there are any copies of the books from which the extracts have been taken for the pupil's page, in case the pupils' appetites for the whole book are sufficiently whetted by the opening page.

Organisation:
(a) The pupils should work in groups of two to four.
(b) Read each extract while the pupils follow it in their books.
(c) Write on the board some general headings to help the group discuss each opening. These might include:

> Are characters introduced?
> Do we know where the story is set?
> Is the language clear?
> What sort of story does it promise to be?
> What is the mood of the piece?
> Do I want to read on?
> Etc.

(d) Have a reporting back session. Ask for comments for and against each opening. If you like, let each group award each extract points out of five to give a score at the end.

Extension:
(a) When pupils are choosing books to read, make sure the insights gained by this activity are used to assess the first page.
(b) Do some similar work using the blurbs which appear on the back or cover-flap or sometimes inside a book.

34 Compare these landscapes

Talk expected: comparative; personal; explanatory.

Objectives:
(a) to talk about the two main kinds of landscape we inhabit and compare their effects on us
(b) to consider the historical process that shaped these landscapes.

Organisation:
(a) The pupils should work in pairs or threes.
(b) Talk in general terms about the two pictures, linking them if possible with the pupils' own personal experience.
(c) Ask groups to discuss the first four questions, making notes of their conclusions, and then have a reporting back session on this.
(d) Ask the pupils to make a sequence chart to show what they think shaped these two landscapes over the centuries and why such changes were necessary. Discuss these in a reporting back session, correcting any errors and writing a correct sequence for each of the two landscapes on the board, using the pupils' contributions.

35 Can you solve this problem?

Talk expected: problem-solving; imaginative; explanatory.

Objective: to provide an opportunity for a problem-solving discussion.

Organisation:
(a) Divide the class into pairs or small groups.
(b) Read the first part of the story aloud while the pupils follow it on their page.
(c) Groups should then try to come up with a solution to the problem. Those who come up with one quickly should be encouraged to think of two solutions.
(d) Have each group who has a solution report back. Record these briefly on the board and then ask each group to consider the solutions in turn and decide which one(s) they like best. Then take a vote.
(e) Read the second half of the story (below) to the pupils. Do they think it contains the best solution?

The Wise Arab – *Part Two*

Pasha coughed. 'Might I suggest,' he said, 'that you accept the gift of another camel from me?'

The brothers turned to the old man and the youngest said, 'But Pasha, you have so little and you have done so much for our family already. We could not think of taking anything else from you.'

Pasha shook his head. 'For your old father's sake – and remember, he was my greatest friend – I will give you my only camel. With that camel you will then have eighteen, an easy number to divide into halves, thirds, and ninths.'

The brothers protested, but Pasha insisted, so finally they accepted his gift with gratitude. They declared that, old as he was, his brain was sharper than theirs, for he had solved their problem.

The eldest son led to one side of the courtyard nine of the camels, which was half.

The middle son led to the other side of the courtyard six camels, this being one third.

The youngest son counted those that were left. There were three. 'How very odd,' he thought. 'Even I know that one ninth of eighteen is two. I should have only two camels, and yet there are three left.' He laughed aloud and called to the others to join him.

The brothers turned to their old friend, the wise Pasha, and said, 'You have been so good to us, surely *you* must have the spare camel. If you will take it, it is yours.'

Pasha did not refuse. He simply smiled, and patted the nose of the camel. It was the very camel that he had given the sons to solve their problem – and he had been sure he would get it back.

36 Teach a friend to tell a story

Talk expected: narrative.

Objectives:
(a) to develop storytelling based upon a text
(b) to develop the skill of sequencing the main events of a story.

Organisation:
(a) Decide how many pairs you want working on this at any one time.
(b) Explain the activity to the pairs, using the guide on the pupil's page.
(c) If you like, ask the pupils to come to you when they have completed point 2 on their page so that you can hear them tell the story using their written sequence of main ideas. Similarly, the second child in the pair can retell the story to you after point 5 on their page.